Chef Bailey's Cherished Recipes

Made Healthier

Retired chef 70, shares his skills

Charles Bailey recently demonstrated the art of cooking to Semmes schoolkids

By JO ANNE McKNIGHT
Correspondent
Article taken from Mobile Press; January 10, 2010; Sally Ericson, Mobile Press Editor

Charles Bailey left Vinegar Bend when he was 15 and did not return to the area for more than half a century.

Now. 70, Bailey finds that althoUgh it's good to 136 home, he wouldrettrade all theme years away for anything.

During hisyears as an award-winning chef, he catered dinners for the Rev. Jesse Jackson and former President Ronald Reagan and Muhammad Ali. He also met South African President Nelson Mandela and former Egyptian President Anwar Sadat.

He developed and marketed his own brand of butter cooking and flavoring. He owned a couple of restaurants and coauthored a book, "15 Master Chefs Reveal their Secrets."

Food preparation is definitely his, calling. With his slight build, he said, he knew even as a youngster that he wasn't meant for a football career.

But cooking appealed to him. He left Washington County for New Orleans and worked with a chef who took him to Algeria.

There he learned the art of ice sculpture and salt carving (statues made from a mixture of salt and corn starch).

Back in New Orleans, Bailey worked for 15 years at a hotel owned by Braniff Airlines. Eventuaily, he became executive chef with 60 employees in his charge.

In the 1970s, his food preparation artistry won him several awards.

Throughout the years, Bailey has owned his own restaurants or has run the food service in others in New Orleans, Baton Rouge and Atlanta.

But then Hurricane Katrina struck. Bailey was among the New Orleans residents rescued by helicopter because of rising flood waters.

Bailey now works at Gilmer Funeral Home in Mobile, where he manages the food preparation, and service for visitations and wakes.

In a recent demonstration for students at Semmes Middle School on Career Day, "I de-boned chickens, showed the students the difference between sauteing and frying, told them about sanitation and about having respect for the cooks," he said He also stressed that cooks should respect their customers.

Bailey also demonstrated how to prepare omelets, chicken and shrimp Alfredo.

Table of Contents

Beverages and Sauces

Russian Spiced Tea

INGREDIENTS

1½ C	Instant *Lipton Tea* with *NutraSweet*
2 Lg boxes	Diet orange gelatin
1 tsp	Cinnamon
¼ tsp	Clove
2-3 pkg	*Equal* or *Sweet & Low* to taste

DIRECTIONS

1. Put 1 teaspoon to 1 Cup hot water.

Breakfast Shake

INGREDIENTS

8 oz	Low-fat plain yogurt
1 C	Skim milk
1	Banana
1 tsp	Vanilla extract
1 pkg	Frozen strawberries, unsweet (14 oz)
3-4 pkt	*Equal* or *Sweet & Low*
½ C	Orange juice, unsweetened*

DIRECTIONS

1. Mix all ingredients in blender on high until smooth.

May substitute 14 oz can unsweetened pineapple (add fruit and juices) for strawberries and orange juice.

Yield: 4
Per Serving: Calories 92; Fat <1 g; Carbs 19 g

Ranch Dip

INGREDIENTS

1¾ C	Plain Low-Fat Yogurt
½ tsp	Garlic Powder
¼ C	Light Mayonnaise
½ tsp	Dill Weed
1 tsp	Dried Parsley Flakes
¼ tsp	Paprika
1 tsp	Dried Minced Onion
¼ tsp	Pepper
½ tsp	Onion Powder
¼ tsp	Celery Powder

DIRECTIONS

1. Place ingredients in mixing bowl. Stir until blended and smooth.
2. Pour into container and refrigerate 1 hour to blend flavors.
3. Can be stored for several weeks. Use on salad greens or as dip for raw vegetables: broccoli, carrots, squash, celery, tomato or seasonal vegetables.

Yield: *32 (2 Cups)*
Per Serving: *Calories 8; Fat <1 g; Carbs 1 g*

Thousand Island Dressing

INGREDIENTS

1 C	Light Mayonnaise
½ C	Catsup
2 tsp	Mustard
2 T	Pickle Relish
1	Egg White From Boiled Egg (Optional)

DIRECTIONS

1. Mix all ingredients.

Yield: *1⅔ C, Serving Size: 1 Tablespoon*
Per Serving: *Calories 34; Fat 2 g; Carbs 3 g*

Bar-B-Q Sauce

INGREDIENTS

1 8oz can	Tomato Sauce
¼ C	Fresh Lemon Juice
1 T	Brown Sugar
2 T	Vinegar
1 T	Worcestershire Sauce
1 T	Prepared Mustard
Dash	Pepper
Dash	Red Pepper
⅛ T	Garlic Powder

DIRECTIONS

1. Combine ingredients in a saucepan. Bring to a boil.
2. Cover and simmer 15-20 minutes on low heat. Excellent to marinate chicken or meats overnight and grill.

Yield: *1⅓ Cups*
Serving Size: *2 Tablespoons*
Per Serving: *Calories 12; Fat 0 g; Carbs 3 g*

Brown Gravy

INGREDIENTS

2 C	Defatted Beef Broth
Dash	Salt
2 T	Cornstarch
Dash	Pepper

DIRECTIONS

1. Save leftover meat broth and place in refrigerator several hours.
2. Skim fat from broth.
3. Place defatted broth over low heat, adding 2 tablespoons cornstarch until thickened. Season to taste.

Serving Size: *2 Tablespoons*
Per Serving: *Calories 2; Fat 0 g; Carbs 0g*

Chef Bailey's Cherished Recipes Made Healthier

Fat Free Roux

Place 1 cup flour in cast iron skillet or Dutch oven. Bake at 400 degrees until dark brown. Stir occasionally.

Microwave Method:

Place 1 cup flour in Pyrex casserole dish. Microwave high for 2 minutes; stir well. Repeat at 2-minute intervals, stirring well until flour is dark brown.

Yield: *1 Cup*
Serving Size: *2 ½ Tablespoons*
Per Serving: *Calories 72; Fat 0 g; Carbs 15 g*

Vegetable Sauce

INGREDIENTS

12 oz	*V-8* (Vegetable Cocktail) Juice
1 T	Corn Starch
¼ C	Chopped Onion
¼ C	Chopped Celery
1 T	Diet Margarine

DIRECTIONS

1. Sauté chopped onion and celery in margarine until tender. Set aside.
2. Add V-8 juice to saucepan over low heat. Add 1 tablespoon corn starch, mixing well. Cook quickly, stirring constantly until thickened.
3. Use over rice and meats as a gravy.

Serving Size: *2 Tablespoons*
Per Serving: *Calories 12; Fat <1 g; Carbs <1 g*

INGREDIENTS

2 T	Margarine
2 T	All-Purpose Flour
¼ tsp	Salt
1 C	Skim Milk

DIRECTIONS

1. Melt margarine in saucepan over low heat.
2. Blend in flour, salt, and dash of white or black pepper.
3. Add milk all at once. Cook quickly, stirring constantly until mixture thickens and bubbles.

Serving Size: *2 Tablespoons*
Per Serving: *Calories 34; Fat 2 g; Carbs 3*

Soups

Potato Soup

INGREDIENTS

6 C	Peeled and Sliced Red Potatoes
4 C	Sliced Onions
1½-2 quarts	Water (just to cover potatoes and onions)
4 tsp	Powdered Chicken Broth or 5 Bouillon Cubes
1 C	Skim Milk
1 bunch	Green Onions, Finely Sliced
	Salt and Pepper to Taste

DIRECTIONS

1. Bring potatoes and onions to boil in water. Reduce heat and simmer, partially covered, for 45 minutes.

2. When potatoes are tender, transfer with onions and water to food processor in batches and process until smooth.

3. Return to pot and add remaining ingredients except green onions, cooking until thoroughly heated. Top with green onions and serve.

Yield: *12 Servings*
Per Serving: *Calories 95; Fat 0.5 g*

Roasted Garlic-Potato Soup

INGREDIENTS

1 C	Fat-free Milk
¼ C	Water
½ pack	(7.6 oz) Package Roasted Garlic Instant Mashed Potatoes
1 C	(4 oz) Pre-shredded Reduced Fat Sharp Cheddar Cheese, Divided
¼ tsp	Freshly Ground Pepper

DIRECTIONS

1. Combine milk and water in a large saucepan; bring to a boil.
2. Remove from heat; add potatoes, and stir with a whisk until well blended.
3. Add ¾ cup cheese, stirring until cheese melts.
4. Spoon evenly into 4 bowls; sprinkle evenly with remaining ¼ cup cheese and pepper.

Yield: *Four 1-Cup Servings*
Per Serving: *Calories 219; Fat 7.6 g; Carbs 25.2 g*

Potato Soup 2

INGREDIENTS

1	Medium Potato, Peeled and Diced
2 T	Chopped Onion
2 T	Sliced Celery
¼ tsp	Instant Chicken Bouillon Granules
⅛ tsp	Dried Basil, Crushed
¼ Cup	Frozen Peas
½ Cup	Skim Milk
1 tsp	Cornstarch

DIRECTIONS

1. In saucepan, combine potato, onion, celery, bouillon, basil, ⅓ cup water, and dash pepper. Bring to boil; reduce heat. Simmer covered 5 minutes.

2. Add peas. Bring to boiling; reduce heat. Simmer covered about 5 minutes more.

3. Combine milk and cornstarch; add to potato mixture. Cook and stir until bubbly. Cook and stir 2 minutes.

4. Place in a microwave safe container. Store in refrigerator up to 2 days. In the morning, pack in an insulated lunch box with a frozen ice pack. To serve, microwave on 100% power (high) about 3 minutes.

Yield: *1 Serving*
Per Serving: *Calories 236; Fat <1 g; Carbs 49 g*

Beefy Vegetable & Barley

INGREDIENTS

2 Lbs	Lean Round Steak, ½ Inch Thick
1	Onion, Chopped
3	Stalks Celery, Chopped
1	Bay Leaf
2 T	Chopped Parsley
2 C	Water
1	(46 oz) Can Cocktail Vegetable Juice
1	Red Potato, Peeled, Cut in Small Cubes
½ Cup	Barley
1	Large Carrot, Sliced
1	(10 oz) Package Frozen Mixed Vegetables

DIRECTIONS

1. Cut meat into 1-inch cubes. Coat a large heavy pot with no stick cooking spray. Add meat, cooking until browned, stirring often.

2. Add onion, celery, bay leaf, parsley, and water. Bring to boil, lower heat and simmer covered 45 min.

3. Add vegetable juice, potato, and barley. Cook 30 minutes and add carrot and mixed vegetables.

4. Cover, and cook over low heat 30 minutes or until meat is tender and barley is done.

Yield: *6 to 8 Servings*
Per Serving: *Calories 257; Fat 5.0 g*

Mediterranean Beef Stew

INGREDIENTS

2	Zucchini, Cut into Bite-Sized Pieces
¾ Lb	Beef Stew Meat, Cut to Half-Inch Pieces
2	(14.5 oz) Cans Italian Style Diced Tomatoes, Un-Drained
½ T	Pepper
1	2 Inch Cinnamon Stick or ¼ Teaspoon Ground Cinnamon

DIRECTIONS

1. Place zucchini in bottom of a 3½ quart electric slow cooker. Add beef and remaining ingredients; stir well.

2. Cover and cook on high heat setting 5 hours or until meat is tender OR cover and cook on high heat setting 1 hour; reduce to low heat setting, and cook 7 hours.

3. Remove and discard cinnamon stick before serving.

Yield: *4 (1½ Cup) Servings*
Per Serving: *Calories 193; Fat 4 g; Carbs 16.9 g*

Turkey Vegetable Soup

INGREDIENTS

	Cooking Spray
1 Lb	Ground Turkey
2 cans	No-Salt-Added Beef Broth, Divided (14 ¼ oz Cans)
¼ C	All-Purpose Flour
1 can	Mexican-Style Stewed Tomatoes, Undrained (14½ oz Cans)
1 pkg	Frozen Vegetable Soup Mix with Tomatoes
¼ tsp	Salt
¼ tsp	Pepper

DIRECTIONS

1. Coat a Dutch oven with cooking spray; place over medium-high heat until hot. Add turkey; cook, stirring constantly, until it crumbles.

2. Combine 1 cup broth and flour, stirring until well blended. Add flour mixture, remaining broth, tomatoes, and remaining ingredients to Dutch oven. Bring to a boil; cover, reduce heat to medium, and cook 20 minutes.

Yield: *4 (2 Cup) Servings*
Per Serving: *Calories 295; Fat 4.3 g; Carbs 29.6 g*

Chicken Soup

INGREDIENTS • Part 1

4 Qt	Water
1 Lb	Chicken Breasts, Boneless, Skinless
1 tsp	Thyme
1	Carrot, Sliced
1 tsp	Basil
1	Onion, Chopped
5 sprigs	Parsley
1 rib	Celery, Chopped
3-4	Peppercorns
1 tsp	Salt
1 clove	Garlic, Minced

DIRECTIONS

1. Cook 1 hour. Skim foam. Refrigerate chicken. Skim fat. Bring broth to a boil and add:

INGREDIENTS • Part 2

1 tsp	Salt
1 tsp	Pepper
3 oz	Noodles
3	Carrots, Sliced
1 C	Onion, Chopped
	Cubed Chicken

DIRECTIONS

2. Simmer until vegetables and noodles are tender.

Yield: *16 (1 Cup) Servings*
Per Serving: *Calories 70; Fat 2 g; Carbs 5 g*

Cheesy Soup

INGREDIENTS

3 T	Liquid Margarine
3½ C	Chicken Broth
½ C	Chopped Onion
½ Lb	Reduced Fat Sharp Cheddar Cheese, Shredded
¼ C	Finely Chopped Celery
½ C	Finely Chopped Carrots
1½ C	Skim Milk
½ C	Finely Chopped Green Bell Pepper
4 T	Chopped Green Onions
3 T	Flour
¼ tsp	Dry Mustard
	Salt and Pepper to Taste

DIRECTIONS

1. In pot melt margarine and sauté onion, carrot, green pepper, and celery until tender.
2. Blend in flour and dry mustard; gradually add chicken broth, mixing until well blended. Bring to a boil and cook until slightly thickened, stirring frequently. Reduce heat and simmer for 10 minutes.
3. Slowly add shredded cheese and cook until melted.

4. Add 1 cup skim milk. Add the remaining 1.2 cup milk only if soup is too thick. Heat and season to taste. Before, serving, sprinkle with green onions.

Yield: 4 Servings
Per Serving: Calories 340; Fat 14.1g

Chef Bailey's Cherished Recipes Made Healthier

Cream of Broccoli Soup

INGREDIENTS

10 oz	Frozen Chopped Broccoli
1 Qt	Skim Milk
Pinch	White Pepper
¼ tsp	Baking Soda
4 cubes	Chicken Bouillon
4 T	Margarine
8 T	Flour

DIRECTIONS

1. In large saucepan, combine broccoli, skim milk, white pepper, baking soda, and chicken bouillon; bring to a boil.
2. Combine margarine and flour in a small skillet, stirring slowly with a wire whisk.
3. When soup has reached desired thickness, return to a light boil for 5 to 8 minutes.

Yield: Eight 1¼-Cup Servings
Per Serving: Calories 169; Fat 5 g; Carbs 20 g

Cream of Tomato Soup

INGREDIENTS

2 C	Canned Crushed Tomatoes
½ C	Diced Onion
½ tsp	Salt
½	Bay Leaf
2 T	Diet Margarine
1 T	Enriched All-Purpose Flour
1 C	Evaporated Skim Milk
Dash	Pepper

DIRECTIONS

1. In one-quart saucepan, combine tomatoes, onion, salt, and bay leaf; bring to a boil. Remove from heat and discard bay leaf.

2. Transfer mixture to a blender container; set aside and allow to cool slightly.

3. In same saucepan, heat margarine over low heat until bubbly. Using a wire whisk, add flour and cook, stirring constantly, until smooth. Gradually stir in milk; continue stirring and cook until thickened. Remove from heat and set aside.

4. Process tomato mixture to milk mixture; add pepper and stir. Reheat soup over low heat before serving, stirring occasionally. (DO NOT BOIL).

Yield: *4 Servings*
Per Serving: *Calories 91; Fat 3 g; Carbs 11 g*

INGREDIENTS

1 T	Diet Margarine
1 can	(10½ oz Can) Condensed Beef Broth
½ C	Broccoli Flowerets
1 soup can	Water
½ C	Sliced Yellow Squash
1 C	Cooked Chicken Cut in 2" Strips
1 C	Mushrooms
¼ C	Sliced Green Onions
1 small clove	Garlic, Minced
1 C	Red Bell Pepper Cut in 1" Strips
⅛ tsp	Dried Thyme Leaves, Crushed

DIRECTIONS

1. In medium saucepan over medium heat, melt margarine. Cook mushrooms in hot margarine until browned.
2. Add garlic, thyme, broccoli, and squash. Cook about 5 minutes until broccoli is just tender, stirring occasionally.
3. Add soup, water, chicken, green onions, and red pepper. Cook 3 minutes or until heated through.

Yield: *2 Servings*
Per Serving: *Calories 215; Fat 11 g; Carbs 10 g*

INGREDIENTS

1 can	Chicken Broth
4 C	Water
2	Medium Onions, Chopped
2	Medium Carrots, Chopped
2 ribs	Celery, Chopped
1 C	Finely-Chopped Parsley
1 cup each	Dried Pinto, Red Kidney, Small White Beans (Rinsed)
3 cloves	Garlic, Minced
1 can	Tomatoes, Chopped
	Salt or Salt Substitute
	Black Pepper
	Freshly Grated Parmesan Cheese (Garnish)

DIRECTIONS

1. Soak beans overnight in plenty of cold water or boil 2 minutes; cover and let stand 1 hour. Drain.
2. Add 1 tablespoon of oil in Dutch oven. Cook, celery and onions 3 minutes, stirring often.
3. Add carrots, broth, water, beans, tomatoes, garlic, ¼ cup parsley, and the bay leaf. Boil uncovered 10 minutes.
4. Reduce heat and simmer uncovered until beans are

tender, about 1 hour.

5. Remove bay leaf. Season with salt and pepper. Stir in remaining ¼ cup parsley. Serve soup with 1 tablespoon of Parmesan cheese.

Yield: *8 Servings*
Per Serving: *Calories 188; Fat <1 g; Carbs 35 g*

INGREDIENTS

1 pkg	(16 oz) Frozen Broccoli, Corn and Red Peppers
3 C	Frozen Potatoes O'Brien with Onions and Peppers
1 can	(14¼ oz) Fat-Free, Low-Sodium Chicken Broth or Vegetable Broth
1 C	Fat-Free Half-and-Half or Evaporated Fat-Free Milk
½ block	(8 oz) Light Processed Cheese, Cubed (Such as Velveeta Light)
¼ tsp	Pepper

DIRECTIONS

1. Combine first 3 ingredients in a large saucepan; bring to a boil. Cover, reduce heat, and simmer 6 minutes or until vegetables are tender.
2. Stir in half-and-half and cheese; continue stirring until cheese melts and soup is thoroughly heated. Stir in pepper, and serve immediately.

Yield: *4 (1½ Cup) Servings*
Per Serving: *Calories 250; Fat 3.6 g; Carbs 39.2 g*

Sandwiches

Vegetarian Chili

INGREDIENTS

1½ C	Chopped Onions
1½ tsp	Minced Garlic
3 cans	(1 Lb) Red Kidney Beans, Rinsed, Drained
1½ C	Tomato Juice
1 can	(4 oz) Chopped Green Chilies, Un-Drained
1	Large Ripe Tomato, Cut to ¼ Inch Pieces
1¼ tsp	Chili Powder
1 tsp	Cumin
½ C	Shredded Reduced Fat Cheddar Cheese
	Salt and Pepper to Taste

DIRECTIONS

1. In large pot, sauté onion and garlic in water. Cover, and cook 10 minutes, stirring, until onion is tender.
2. Stir in remaining ingredients except cheese. Cook for 5 to 10 minutes until hot.
3. Serve in bowls with shredded cheese.

Yield: *6 Servings*
Per Serving: *Calories 195; Fat 1.5g*

Hot Beef & Pepper Rolls

INGREDIENTS

½ Lb	Thinly Sliced Deli Roast Beef, Cut into Strips
1	Large Red Bell Pepper, Thinly Sliced
1	Large Green Bell Pepper, Thinly Sliced
1	Large Onion, Thinly Sliced
4	(2.8 oz) Steak Rolls, Split and Warmed
½ tsp	Dried Oregano (Optional)

DIRECTIONS

1. Coat a large nonstick skillet with cooking spray; place over medium-high heat until hot.
2. Add meat, peppers, and onion; sauté until meat is hot and onion is tender.
3. Spoon meat mixture evenly onto bottom halves of rolls.
4. Sprinkle with oregano, if desired, and top with remaining roll halves.

Yield: *4 Servings*
Per Serving: *Calories 321; Fat 4.8 g; Carbs 53.8 g*

Saucy Dogs

INGREDIENTS

½ Lb	Ground Round
1 C	Chopped Onion
1 can	(15 oz) Sloppy-Joe Sauce
8	Low-Fat Frankfurters
8	Hot Dog Buns

DIRECTIONS

1. Combine beef and onion in a nonstick skillet over medium-high heat. Cook until beef is browned and onion is tender, stirring until meat crumbles. Drain, if necessary, and return to skillet.

2. Add Sloppy-Joe sauce to beef mixture, and bring to a boil. Reduce heat, and simmer for 5 minutes, stirring occasionally.

3. While sauce cooks, cook frankfurters according to package directions: Place 1 frankfurter in each bun.

4. Spoon beef mixture evenly over frankfurter.

Yield: *8 Servings*
Per Serving: *Calories 278; Fat 6.6 g; Carbs 36.2 g*

INGREDIENTS

¾ **Lb**	Ground Turkey Breast
1	Onion, Chopped
1 can	(8 oz) No-Salt Added Tomato Sauce
1 bottle	(7 oz) Roasted Bell Peppers, Drained and Chopped
¼ **tsp**	Salt
¼ **tsp**	Pepper
2 T	Liquid Mesquite Smoke (Optional)
4	(2.25 oz) Whole Wheat or Plain Kaiser Rolls

DIRECTIONS

1. Cook turkey and onion in a non-stick skillet over medium-high heat for 4 to 5 minutes or until onion is tender and turkey is done; stir until turkey crumbles.

2. Stir in tomato sauce and red peppers; simmer 5 minutes.

3. Stir in salt, pepper, and if desired, liquid smoke.

4. Spoon turkey mixture evenly onto bottom halves of rolls, and top with remaining roll halves.

Yield: *4 Servings*
Per Serving: *Calories 346; Fat 5.2 g; Carbs 45.6 g*

Vegetables & Sides

Taco-Chicken Tortilla Wraps

INGREDIENTS

4	(8-Inch) Fat-Free Flour Tortillas
1 Lb	Chicken Breast Tenders
1 pkg	(1.25-oz) 40%-Less Sodium Taco Seasoning Mix
1 C	Thinly Sliced Onion
2 C	Shredded Iceberg Lettuce
1	Ripe Tomato, Chopped
½ C	Fat-Free Sour Cream
	Cooking Spray

DIRECTIONS

1. Preheat oven to 375°.
2. Wrap tortillas in aluminum foil; bake at 375' for 10 minutes or until thoroughly heated.
3. While tortillas bake, combine chicken and taco seasoning in a heavy duty, zip-top plastic bag. Seal bag; shake well.
4. Coat a large nonstick skillet with cooking spray; place over medium-high heat until hot. Add chicken and onion; sauté 6 minutes or until chicken is done. *Continues...*

5. Spoon chicken mixture evenly down center of each tortilla; top evenly with lettuce, tomato and sour cream. Roll up tortillas. Serve immediately.

Yield: *4 Servings*
Per Serving: *Calories 299; Fat 1.8 g; Carbs 36.3 g*

Carrots With Flair

INGREDIENTS

8	Carrots (Medium Size)
1 slice	Whole Wheat Bread
⅓ C	Chopped Onion
½ T	Light Margarine
½ C	Light Mayonnaise
	Paprika
2 T	Horseradish
⅛ tsp	Pepper

DIRECTIONS

1. Peel and slice carrots in julienne (slender short strips) strips.
2. Place in microwave dish and add 1 cup water. Cover and cook in microwave approximately 5 minutes or until tender. Drain, reserving 1/4 cup liquid.
3. Place carrots in a shallow 1 1/2 —quart casserole coated with no stick cooking spray.
4. Combine reserved carrot liquid, onion, mayonnaise, horseradish, and pepper. Spoon over top of carrots.
5. Place bread in food processor until turns into crumbs.
6. Stir in margarine and sprinkle over top of carrots.

7. Sprinkle with paprika. Bake, uncovered, 15 to 20 minutes.

Yield: *6 Servings*
Per Serving: *Calories 110; Fat 7.2 g*

Orange Glazed Carrots

INGREDIENTS

2 Lb	Baby Carrots or Carrots Cut into 2" Pieces
2 T	Light Margarine
¼ C	Chicken Broth
1 C	Orange Marmalade
2 T	Chopped Parsley
	Salt and Pepper to Taste

DIRECTIONS

1. Peel carrots.
2. In saucepan, bring the margarine and broth to boil. Add the carrots and cook, covered, over medium heat for 10 to 20 minutes, until crisp tender.
3. Uncover and stir in marmalade. Cook, stirring, over low heat until liquid has reduced to a glaze. Season to taste. Garnish with parsley before serving.

Yield: *8-10 Servings*
Per Serving: *Calories 133; Fat 1.4 g*

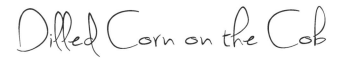
Dilled Corn on the Cob

INGREDIENTS

4 ears (6") Frozen Corn
Butter-Flavored Spray (such as *I Can't Believe It's Not Butter*)
Minced Fresh or Dried Dill

DIRECTIONS

1. Prepare grill.
2. Coat ears of corn with butter-flavored spray, sprinkle with dill.
3. Place corn on grill rack, and grill, uncovered, 20 minutes or until corn is tender, turning occasionally.

Yield: *4 Servings*
Per Serving: *Calories 73; Fat 1.2 g; Carbs: 15.7 g*

Marinated Green Beans

INGREDIENTS

1 Lb	Fresh Green Beans
2 T	Peanut Oil
2 T	Olive Oil
2 T	Vinegar
¼ tsp	Garlic Powder
1 T	Prepared Mustard
½ tsp	Crushed Rosemary

DIRECTIONS

1. Cook green beans for 10 minutes. Drain.
2. Combine remaining ingredients and pour over beans.
3. Marinate overnight.
4. Serve cold.

Yield: *8 (½ Cup) Servings*
Per Serving: *Calories 91; Fat 7 g; Carbs 5 g*

Green Beans & Potatoes In Cream Sauce

INGREDIENTS

4 C	Fresh Green Beans
8	Small New Red Potatoes
2 C	Skim Milk
2 T	Cornstarch
2 pkg	Butter Buds
	Pepper to Taste

DIRECTIONS

1. Cook green beans and potatoes in large pot with 1-2 quarts water.
2. Dissolve 2 pkgs. Butter buds with 1 cup hot water and add to green beans. Additional water may be added if needed. Green beans and potatoes should be tender.
3. Mix ¼ cup skim milk with 2 T cornstarch. Add this mixture to remaining skim milk.
4. Pour skim milk mixture into green beans and potatoes. Cook until thickened to desired consistency. Add pepper to taste.

Yield: *8 Servings*
Per Serving: *Calories 100; Fat <1 g; Carbs 21 g*

Skillet Beans & Tomatoes

INGREDIENTS

1 pkg	(10 oz) Frozen Cut Green Beans
½ C	Coarsely Chopped Onion
1 tsp	Sugar
¼ tsp	Salt
¼ tsp	Pepper
2	Ripe Tomatoes, Cut into Chunks
	Cooking Spray

DIRECTIONS

1. Combine green beans, onion, sugar, salt, and pepper in a large no-stick skillet coated with cooking spray. Cover and cook over medium heat 8 minutes, stirring occasionally.
2. Add tomatoes; cover and cook 2 minutes or until thoroughly heated.

Yield: 4 (¾ cup) Servings
Per Serving: Calories 47; Fat .4 g; Carbs 10.5 g

Buttery Snow Peas

INGREDIENTS

2 pkg   (6 oz) Frozen Snow Peas
1 T   Yogurt-Based Spread (Such as *Brummel & Brown*)

DIRECTIONS

1. Place snow peas in a microwave-safe bowl. Microwave at HIGH 3 to 4 minutes or until crisp-tender.
2. Add spread, stirring until melted.

Yield: 4 (½ Cup) Servings
Per Serving: Calories 46; Fat 1.5 g; Carbs 6.1 g

Steamed Red Potatoes

INGREDIENTS

1 Lb	Red Potatoes, Quartered
2 T	Water
¼ tsp	Salt
¼ tsp	Pepper
	Butter-Flavored Spray (Such as *I Can't Believe It's Not Butter*)

DIRECTIONS

1. Place potatoes in a microwave-safe dish. Add water, and cover. microwave at HIGH 8 minutes or until tender.
2. Coat with butter-flavored spray, and sprinkle with salt and pepper.

Yield: *4 Servings*
Per Serving: *Calories 86; Fat .3 g; Carbs 18.9 g*

INGREDIENTS

6	Medium Potatoes, Cooked
¼ C	Green Onion, Chopped
¼ C	Celery, Chopped
3	Medium Pimentos, Chopped
¾ C	Light Mayonnaise
1 tsp	Mustard
4	Egg Whites, Cubed from Hard Boiled Egg
¼ tsp	Salt (Optional)
¼ C	Sweet Pickle Relish
	Paprika

DIRECTIONS

1. Peel and cube potatoes.
2. Mix potatoes with green onion, celery, pimento, and cubed egg whites.
3. Blend mayonnaise, mustard, and salt.
4. Toss vegetables with sauce.
5. Sprinkle with paprika.

Yield: *16 (½ Cup) Servings*
Per Servings: *Calories 96; Fat 4 g; Carbs 13 g*

Mexican Stuffed Potatoes

INGREDIENTS

4	Baking Potatoes (Approx. 1½ Lbs)
¼ C	Skim Milk
1	(8 oz) Container Non-Fat Yogurt
⅛ tsp	Black Pepper
¼ C	Shredded Reduced Fat Monterey Jack Cheese
½ C	Shredded Reduced Fat Cheddar Cheese, Divided
1 can	(4 oz) Diced Green Chilies, Drained
1 jar	(2 oz) Diced Pimiento, Drained
2	Large Green Onion Stems, Thinly Sliced

DIRECTIONS

1. Wash potatoes well and dry thoroughly. With fork, prick skins over entire surface. Place potatoes directly on oven rack, and bake at 400 degrees for 1 hour or until soft when squeezed. Let cool to touch.

2. Cut potatoes in half lengthwise; carefully scoop out pulp, leaving a thin shell. Set aside.

3. In mixing bowl, combine potato pulp, yogurt, milk, and pepper, mixing until light and fluffy.

4. Stir in green onion stems, chilies, pimiento, and ¼ cup each cheese into potato mixture.

5. Fill potato shells with mashed potato mixture. Sprinkle with remaining ¼ cup shredded Cheddar cheese. Bake at 350 degrees for approximately 20 minutes or until cheese is melted and potatoes are hot.

Yield: *8 Servings*
Per Serving: *Calories 123; Fat 0.9 g*

Potato Bake

INGREDIENTS

2 Lb	Potatoes, Unpeeled and Sliced
1	Red Bell Pepper, Chopped
1	Bunch Green Onions, Chopped
1	Green Bell Pepper Chopped
3 T	Olive Oil
1 tsp	Paprika
1 can	(14½ oz) Reduced Salt Chicken Broth
	Salt and Pepper to Taste
2 T	Dried Basil
6 cloves	Garlic, Minced

DIRECTIONS

1. Combine all ingredients, tossing to coat well.
2. Place potato mixture in a 13x9x2-inch baking dish. Bake at 325 degrees for 1 hour and 15 minutes or until potatoes are tender and liquid is absorbed.

Yield: *6 Servings*
Per Serving: *Calories 206; Fat 7.5 g*

Cheesy Stuffed Potato

INGREDIENTS

1	Medium Baking Potato
1 can	(6½ oz) Water-Packed Chicken, Drained and Flaked
1 T	Minced Onion
1 T	Finely Chopped Celery
1 T	Finely Chopped Green Pepper
3 T	Reduced Calorie Mayonnaise
¼ tsp	Seasoned Pepper
2 T	Shredded Low-Fat Cheddar Cheese
	Paprika

DIRECTIONS

1. Wash potato, bake at 375 degrees for 45 to 60 minutes or until done. Let stand until cool enough to handle.

2. Cut potato in half lengthwise; scoop out pulp, leaving a ¼ inch thick shell.

3. Mash potato pulp in a medium bowl with a potato masher or fork; stir in next 6 ingredients, mixing well.

4. Divide mixture evenly into potato shells. Sprinkle each with paprika. Place on a baking sheet, bake at 350 degrees for 10 minutes. *Continues...*

5. Remove from oven and sprinkle with cheese. Bake an additional 5 minutes or until thoroughly heated.

Yield: *2 Servings*
Per Serving: *Calories 233; Fat 9 g; Carbs 15 g*

INGREDIENTS

½ pkg	(22 oz) Frozen Mashed Potatoes (about 2⅔ cups)
1⅓ C	Fat-Free Milk
¼ tsp	Salt
¼ tsp	Pepper
¼ tsp	Garlic Powder

DIRECTIONS

1. Combine frozen potatoes, milk, salt, pepper, and garlic powder in a 1½ quart microwave-safe baking dish.
2. Cook according to package microwave directions.

Yield: *4 (⅔ cup) Servings*
Per Serving: *Calories 141; Fat 2.4 g; Carbs 24 g*

Brown Sugar Sweet Potatoes

INGREDIENTS

1 can	(14½ oz) Mashed Sweet Potatoes
2 T	Brown Sugar
1 T	Reduced-Calorie Margarine
2 T	Orange Juice
¼ tsp	Salt

DIRECTIONS

1. Combine sweet potatoes, brown sugar, margarine, orange juice, and salt in a saucepan.
2. Cook over medium heat 5 minutes or until smooth and thoroughly heated, stirring often. Stir in 2 to 3 tablespoons water, if necessary.

Yield: *4 (½ cup) Servings*
Per Serving: *Calories 144; Fat 2.1 g; Carbs 30.2 g*

INGREDIENTS

1 pkg	(10 oz) Frozen Chopped Spinach
1 C	Non-Fat Plain Yogurt
⅔ C	Light Mayonnaise
1 tsp	Seasoned Salt
½ tsp	Dried Dill Weed
½ C	Chopped Parsley
½ C	Chopped Green Onion
	Juice of Half Lemon

DIRECTIONS

1. Thaw, squeeze, and drain chopped spinach.
2. Blend spinach with remaining ingredients in bowl. Refrigerate, Recipe is best when made a day ahead. Serve with fresh vegetables.

Yield: *3 Cups*
Per Serving: *Calories 13; Fat 0.9 g*

Vegetable Skillet

INGREDIENTS

2 C	Thinly Sliced Yellow Squash
4	Tomato Wedges
1 C	Carrots, Sliced Diagonally
½ C	Chopped Onion
½	Bias-Sliced Celery
2 C	Cabbage, Thinly Sliced
1 C	Sliced Mushrooms
½ tsp	Garlic Powder
	Dash Pepper
2 T	Vegetable Oil

DIRECTIONS

1. In large skillet, cook squash, carrots, onion, celery, cabbage, mushrooms, and garlic powder covered in hot oil over medium-high heat 4 minutes, stirring occasionally.

2. Add tomato wedges and pepper. Cook 2 to 3 minutes or until heated through. Serve immediately.

Yield: *8 Servings*
Per Serving: *Calories 75; Fat 3 g; Carbs 9 g*

INGREDIENTS

2	Large Yellow Squash
2	Large Zucchini
1 tsp	Dried Dill
½ tsp	Grated Lemon Rind
¼ tsp	Salt
1 T	Lemon Juice

DIRECTIONS

1. Cut squash and zucchini crosswise into ¼-inch-thick slices:
2. Cook in a large skillet in a small amount of boiling water 3 to 5 minutes or until crisp-tender; drain.
3. Add remaining ingredients, and toss.

Yield: *4 (¾ cup) Servings*
Per Serving: *Calories 34; Fat .2 g; Carbs: 7.4 g*

Southern Blackeyed Peas

INGREDIENTS

4 C	Blackeyed Peas
2 Qt	Water
¼ tsp	Salt
2 oz	Lean Ham, Cubed

DIRECTIONS

1. Place peas in large pot containing 2 quarts water.
2. Add salt and lean ham. Cook approximately 1 hour or until peas are tender. Additional water may be added during cooking.

Dried peas may be used; soak over night or at least 6 hours in cold water. Canadian bacon may be substituted for ham.

Yield: *8 Servings Per ½ Cup*
Per Serving: *Calories 90; Fat <1 g; Carbs 15 g*

Baked Beans in a Pot

INGREDIENTS

1 can	(15 oz) No-Salt-Added Kidney or Pinto Beans, Drained
3 T	Brown Sugar
2 T	Dried Onion Flakes
¼ C	Barbecue Sauce

DIRECTIONS

1. Combine all ingredients in a saucepan. Bring to a boil; cover, reduce heat, and simmer 5 minutes.
2. Uncover and cook 5 minutes.

Yield: *4 (¾ cup) Servings*
Per Serving: *Calories: 128; Fat .6 g; Carbs 25.1 g*

Easy Red Beans and Rice

INGREDIENTS

1 Lb	Ground Turkey Sausage
¼ C	Chopped Bell Pepper
¼ C	Chopped Celery
¼ C	Chopped Green Onion
1 tsp	Each: Garlic Powder, Oregano, Red Pepper, Black Pepper
1 can	Red Beans
1 can	Beef Broth
1 C	Minute Rice

DIRECTIONS

1. Brown ground turkey sausage.
2. Add vegetables, cook 2-3 minutes.
3. Stir in dry seasonings. Add broth and beans. Bring to a rolling boil.
4. Add rice, cover, let set 5-10 minutes.

Yield: *6 Servings (1½ Cups)*
Per Serving: *Calories 308; Fat 8 g; Carbs 31 g*

INGREDIENTS

1 can	(15 oz) No-Salt-Added Kidney or Pinto Beans, Drained
3 T	Brown Sugar
2 T	Dried Onion Flakes
¼ C	Barbecue Sauce

DIRECTIONS

1. Combine all ingredients in a saucepan. Bring to a boil; cover, reduce heat, and simmer 5 minutes.
2. Uncover and cook 5 minutes.

Yield: *4 (¾ Cup) Servings*
Per Serving: *Calories 128; Fat .6 g; Carbs 25.1 g*

White Beans

INGREDIENTS

1 Lb	Navy or Pea Beans
½	Green Pepper, Chopped
1	Onion, Chopped
3 stalks	Celery, Chopped
3	Bay Leaves
4 cloves	Garlic, Minced
½ C	Diced Prosciutto
	Salt and Pepper to Taste
1 T	Olive Oil
2 T	Garlic Powder
1 T	Worcestershire Sauce
2 T	Light Brown Sugar, Optional

DIRECTIONS

1. Soak beans overnight in water. Rinse and drain.
2. In pot coated with no stick cooking spray, sauté green pepper, celery, onion, and garlic in olive oil until tender.
3. Add water to cover. Add remaining ingredients. Bring to a boil, lower heat, and simmer, covered, for 2 hours or until beans are tender.

Yield: 6 servings
Per Serving: Calories 338; Fat: 4.3 g

Rice and Noodles

INGREDIENTS

1 C	Raw Rice
1 T	Light Margarine
1 C	Medium Noodles
2¾ C	Chicken Broth
	Salt and Pepper to Taste

DIRECTIONS

1. In heavy saucepan coated with no stick cooking spray, brown rice in margarine.
2. Add remaining ingredients. Bring mixture to boil, lower heat and simmer, covered, for 20 minutes.

Yield: *6 Servings*
Per Serving: *Calories: 181; Fat: 2.6 g*

Garden Rice Casserole

INGREDIENTS

1 T	Light Margarine, Melted
3 C	Chicken Broth
1½ C	Raw Brown Rice
⅔ C	Shredded Reduced Fat Monterey Jack Cheese
⅔ C	Shredded Reduced Fat Cheddar Cheese
1 T	Olive Oil
2 C	Carrot Julienne Strips, Thin
1	Large Onion, Chipped
2 cloves	Garlic, Minced
½ bunch	Broccoli, Flowerets Only
1 head	Cauliflower, Flowerets Only

DIRECTIONS

1. In large 2-quart casserole, mix margarine, rice, onion, and chicken broth.

2. Cover and bake at 350 degrees for 20 minutes or until rice is done. Remove from oven and stir in thyme.

3. Heat olive in skillet coated with no stick cooking spray and sauté remaining vegetables until crisp tender. Pour over rice mixture. Cover and continue baking for 15 minutes.

4. Combine cheeses and sprinkle over the casserole. Return to oven and bake another 5 minutes or until cheese is melted.

Yield: *6 Servings*
Per Serving: *Calories 363; Fat 7.6 g*

Southwestern Rice

INGREDIENTS

1	Onion, Chopped
2 T	Light Margarine
2 cans	(4 oz) Diced Green Chilies
5 C	Cooked Rice
2 C	Non-Fat Plain Yogurt
1 C	Low Fat Cottage Cheese
6 oz	Reduced Fat Sharp Cheddar Cheese, Shredded
	Salt and Pepper to Taste

DIRECTIONS

1. Sauté onion in margarine until tender.
2. Combine with all ingredients except cheese.
3. Place into a 2-quart casserole dish. Cover with shredded cheese. Bake at 350 degrees for 20 minutes.

Yield: 10 Servings
Per Serving: Calories 218; Fat 2.8 g

Wild Rice and Peppers

INGREDIENTS

1 box	(6 oz) Long Grain and Wild Rice
1	Green Bell Pepper, Sliced Long Thin
½ Lb	Mushrooms, Sliced Long Thin
½ C	Cooked Rice
⅛ C	Olive Oil
1 bunch	Green Onions, Chopped
1	Red Bell Pepper, Sliced Long Thin

DIRECTIONS

1. Cook wild rice according to directions on package.
2. In casserole dish combine wild rice and cooked rice.
3. In skillet, heat olive oil and sauté peppers, mushrooms, and green onions until tender. Fold into rice mixture.

Yield: *8 Servings*
Per Serving: *Calories 126; Fat 3.6 g*

Crawfish Dip

INGREDIENTS

¼ C	Light Margarine
1 can	(10 oz) Chopped Tomatoes and Green Chilies
¼ C	Flour
1 tsp	Worcestershire Sauce
2 cloves	Garlic, Minced
1 Lb	Crawfish Tails, Rinsed and Drained
1	Small Onion, Chopped
1 bunch	Green Onions, Chopped
1 can	(10¾ oz) 99% Fat Free Cream of Mushroom Soup
	Salt and Pepper to Taste

DIRECTIONS

1. In skillet, melt margarine, add flour, and mix well.
2. Sauté all vegetables until tender, stirring constantly, to prevent sticking.
3. Add mushroom soup and chopped tomatoes and green chilies; mix well.
4. Add seasonings. Gently stir in crawfish tails. Cook until dip is thoroughly heated. Serve warm with melba rounds.

Yield: *Approximately 4 Cups*
Per Serving: *Calories 15; Fat 0.5 g*

INGREDIENTS

36	Fresh Medium Mushrooms
1	Onion, Chopped
½ bunch	Green Onions, Chopped
¼ C	Chopped Green Bell Pepper
¼ C	Light Margarine
1 T	Sherry
1 C	Breadcrumbs, Approximately
½ tsp	White Pepper
¼ tsp	Red Pepper
½ tsp	Garlic Powder
	Salt and Pepper to Taste
1 Lb	Crawfish Tails, Rinsed and Drained
2 T	Olive Oil

DIRECTIONS

1. Wash mushrooms and remove stems. Chop stems; set aside.

2. Sauté onions, green onions, and green pepper in margarine in skillet until tender.

3. Add breadcrumbs, chopped mushroom stems, seasonings, and crawfish tails. Mix together and cook over low heat for 15 minutes, stirring occasionally.

4. Add olive oil and sherry.

5. Place mushrooms in metal colander over pot of boiling water. Cover with lid. Cook mushrooms for about 15 minutes. Remove and submerge in ice water. Drain and stuff.

Yield: *36 Mushrooms*
Per Serving: *Calories 44; Fat 1.7 g*

INGREDIENTS

1 pkg	(6 oz) Long Grain and Wild Rice
1 T	Light Margarine
½ C	Pearl Barley
⅓ C	Sliced Almonds, Toasted
3 C	Chicken Broth

DIRECTIONS

1. In saucepan, combine rice, seasoning packet, barley, chicken broth, and margarine. Bring to a boil.

2. Reduce heat, cover, and simmer for 10 minutes.

3. Spoon into a 1 1/2 quart casserole dish. Bake, covered, at 325 degrees for 1 hour or until rice and barley are tender and liquid is absorbed. Fluff rice mixture with a fork; stir in almonds.

Yield: *6-8 Servings*
Per Serving: *Calories 182; Fat 5.2 g*

INGREDIENTS

1 pkg	(16 oz) Broccoli Slaw
1	Red Delicious Apple, Chopped
1	Green Onion, Chopped
½ C	Cider Vinegar
¼ C	Apple Juice
⅓ C	Sugar
¼ tsp	Salt
¼ tsp	Pepper

DIRECTIONS

1. Combine broccoli slaw, apple and green onion in a large bowl.
2. Combine vinegar, apple juice, sugar, salt and pepper, stirring well. Pour vinegar mixture over slaw mixture, and toss. Serve Immediately, or cover and chill.

Yield: *9 (1 Cup) Servings*
Per Serving: *Calories 60; Fat .1 g; Carb: 14.7 g*

Poultry

Salsa Chicken with Pasta

INGREDIENTS

8 oz	Wagon Wheel Pasta, Uncooked
1 jar	(24 oz) Thick and Chunky Mild Salsa
1 pkg	(9 oz) Frozen Cooked Diced Chicken Breast
½ C	(2 oz) Shredded Reduced-Fat Monterey Jack Cheese

DIRECTIONS

1. Cook pasta according to package directions, omitting salt and fat.
2. While pasta cooks, combine salsa and chicken in a medium nonstick skillet. Cover and cook over medium heat 5 minutes or until chicken is thoroughly heated, stirring occasionally.
3. Place 1 cup drained pasta on each of 4 plates; top evenly with chicken mixture and cheese.

Yield: *4 Servings*
Per Serving: *Calories 395; Fat 6.2 g; Carbs 51 g*

Chicken Alfredo Pasta

INGREDIENTS

5½ oz	Rotini, Uncooked (2 Cups)
1 pkg	(10 oz) Frozen Mixed Vegetables, Thawed
1 pkg	(9 oz) Frozen Cooked Diced Chicken Breast, Thawed
1 C	Light Alfredo Sauce or Parmesan and Mozzarella Sauce
¼ C	Shredded Parmesan Cheese
½ tsp	Salt
¼ tsp	Freshly Ground Pepper

DIRECTIONS

1. Cook pasta and vegetables together in boiling water in a Dutch oven 10 minutes or until pasta is done and vegetables are tender.
2. Drain pasta and vegetables; return to Dutch oven.
3. Add chicken and next 3 ingredients to pasta mixture, stirring well. Cook over low heat 2 minutes or until thoroughly heated. Sprinkle with freshly ground pepper.

Yield: 6 (1 Cup) Servings
Per Serving: Calories 225; Fat 6.3 g; Carbs 21.8 g

Chicken Cacciatore

INGREDIENTS

1 pkg	(9 oz) Refrigerated Angel Hair Pasta
	Olive Oil-Flavored Cooking Spray
1 pkg	(18 oz) Frozen Cooked Diced Chicken Breast
1	Green Bell Pepper, Cut into 1" Pieces (About 1 Cup)
1	Small Onion, Cut into 1" Pieces (About 1 Cup)
1 can	(15 oz) Chunky Italian-Style Tomato Sauce
⅔ C	Water
¼ tsp	Pepper

DIRECTIONS

1. Cook pasta according to package directions, omitting salt and fat.
2. While pasta cooks, coat a large nonstick skillet with cooking spray; place over medium-high heat until hot. Add chicken, green pepper, and onion; sauté until chicken is browned and vegetables are crisp-tender.
3. Stir in tomato sauce, water, and and ¼ teaspoon pepper. Reduce heat, and simmer, uncovered, 5 minutes, stirring often.

4. Place ¾ cup drained pasta on each of 5 plates; top each serving with 1 cup chicken mixture.

Yield: 5 servings
Per Serving: Calories 416; Fat 6.1g; Carbs 47.1 g

Chef Bailey's Cherished Recipes Made Healthier

Oven Fried Chicken

INGREDIENTS

18	Saltine Cracker Squares, Crushed
¼ C	Evaporated Skim Milk
2 T	Grated Parmesan Cheese
1 T	Vegetable Oil
6	(4 oz) Skinless, Boneless Chicken Breasts
¾ tsp	Pepper
½ tsp	Each: Basil, Celery Seed, Onion Powder, Oregano, Paprika
⅜ tsp	Salt

DIRECTIONS

1. Combine cracker crumbs, cheese, pepper, basil, celery seed, onion powder, oregano, paprika, and salt in bowl.
2. Dip chicken in evaporated milk and then coat with crumb mixture.
3. Place in lightly greased shallow roasting pan. Bake in 400 degree oven for 30 minutes. Brush with oil and bake 10 minutes longer.

Yield: *6 Servings*
Per Serving: *Calories 210; Fat 6 g; Carbs 9 g*

Three Cheese Chicken Bake

INGREDIENTS

8 oz	Lasagna Noodles
½ C	Chopped Onion
½ C	Chopped Green Pepper
1 can	(10 ³/4 oz) Condensed Cream of Chicken or Turkey Soup
1 can	(4 oz) Sliced Mushrooms, Drained
6 oz	Liteline American Cheese
⅓ C	Skim Milk
½ tsp	Dried Basil
1½ C	Low-Fat Cottage Cheese
8 oz	Chopped Cooked Chicken
½ C	Chopped Pimento
½ C	Grated Parmesan Cheese

DIRECTIONS

1. Cook lasagna noodles in boiling water according to package directions; drain well.
2. In saucepan, cook onion and green pepper in small amount of water until tender; drain, add soup, mushrooms, pimento, milk, and basil to vegetables

in saucepan.

3. Lay half the noodles in a 13x9x2-inch baking pan. Top with half each of the soup mixture, cottage cheese, chopped chicken, American cheese, and Parmesan cheese. Repeat layers of noodles, soup mixture, cottage cheese, and chicken.

4. Bake covered in a 350-degree oven for 45 minutes.

5. Top with remaining American and parmesan cheese. Bake uncovered 2 minutes more or until cheese is melted.

Yield: *9 Servings*
Per Serving: *Calories 195; Fat 7g; Carbs 16gm*

Chicken Breasts with Artichokes and Mushrooms

INGREDIENTS

2 Lb	Skinless, Boneless Chicken Breasts
1 bunch	Green Onions, Chopped
	Onion Powder and Lots of Paprika
2 cloves	Garlic, Minced
	Salt and Pepper to Taste
2 T	Light Margarine
1 can	(14 oz) Artichoke Hearts, Drained
2 T	Flour
½ Lb	Fresh Mushrooms, Sliced
⅔ C	Chicken Broth
3 T	Sherry

DIRECTIONS

1. Season chicken heavily with onion powder, paprika, and salt and pepper. Place chicken in bottom of a 3-quart casserole.

2. Cut artichoke hearts and place around chicken. In small skillet coated with no stick cooking spray, sauté mushrooms, green onions, and garlic until tender.

3. Place mushroom mixture on top of chicken. In same skillet, melt margarine and add flour, stirring. Gradually add chicken broth and sherry, cooking until smooth. Pour sauce over all in casserole.

4. Bake, covered, at 350 degrees for 1 hour. Remove cover, and continue baking for 15 minutes to brown chicken.

Yield: *8 Servings*
Per Serving: *Calories 179; Fat 3.2 g*

Chicken Nuggets

INGREDIENTS

⅓ C	Honey
1 tsp	Cinnamon
½ C	Dry Sherry
2 cloves	Garlic, Minced
2 T	Lemon Juice
1½ Lb	Boneless, Skinless Chicken Breasts, Cubed
1 tsp	Ginger

DIRECTIONS

1. Combine honey, sherry, lemon juice, ginger, cinnamon, and garlic in a zip-top plastic bag.
2. Add chicken cubes, seal, and marinate overnight in pan coated with no stick cooking spray.
3. Broil for 5 minutes or until done, basting with marinade. Serve with toothpicks.

Per Serving: Calories 19; Fat 0.1 g

Chicken Breasts Diane

INGREDIENTS

6	Large Skinless, Boneless Chicken Breasts
1	Lemon, Juiced
	Salt and Pepper to Taste
2 T	Chopped Parsley
1 T	Olive Oil
1 T	Dijon Mustard
1 bunch	Green Onions, Chopped
⅓ C	Chicken Broth

DIRECTIONS

1. Place chicken breasts between sheets of waxed paper and pound slightly with mallet to flatten. Sprinkle with salt and pepper, if desired.
2. In large skillet, heat olive oil. Cook chicken for several minutes on each side until done. Remove from skillet and set aside.
3. Add green onions, lemon juice, parsley, and mustard to pan.
4. Cook, stirring constantly, for 1 minute.
5. Whisk in broth and stir until smooth. Pour sauce over chicken and serve immediately.

Yield: *6 Servings*
Per Serving: *Calories 163; Fat 4 g*

INGREDIENTS

⅓ C	Olive Oil
2 cloves	Garlic, Minced
⅓ C	Sherry
1 tsp	Dried Rosemary
1 T	Fresh Lemon Juice
4	Skinless, Boneless Chicken Breasts
⅓ C	Finely Chopped Onion
	Pepper to Taste

DIRECTIONS

1. In small bowl, whisk together olive oil, sherry, lemon juice, onion, garlic, rosemary, and pepper.
2. Place chicken in a shallow glass dish and pour marinade over.
3. Cover and refrigerate 2 to 4 hours.
4. Broil or grill chicken until done, basting with marinade.

Yield: *4 Servings*
Per Serving: *Calories 329; Fat 20.9 g*

Company Chicken

INGREDIENTS

8	Boneless Skinless Chicken Breasts or Thighs
2 cloves	Garlic, Minced
½ Lb	Fresh Mushrooms, Sliced
	Salt and Pepper to Taste
½ C	White Wine
2 T	Olive Oil
1 can	(28 oz) Tomatoes, Slightly Chopped
1 bunch	Green Onions, Chopped
½ C	Chicken Broth

DIRECTIONS

1. Season chicken breasts with salt and pepper. In large skillet coated with no stick cooking spray, heat olive oil and brown chicken pieces. Remove from pan and set aside.

2. Add green onions, garlic, and mushrooms, and sauté until tender.

3. Add white wine, tomatoes, and broth. Bring to boil, adjust seasonings, and reduce to simmer.

4. Add the chicken, cover, and continue to cook for about 30 to 40 minutes, or until chicken is tender.

Yield: *8 Servings*
Per Serving: *Calories 206; Fat 5.4 g*

INGREDIENTS

2 T	Light Margarine
2 C	Chicken Broth
⅓ C	Chopped Mushrooms
1 C	Evaporated Skimmed Milk
1	Green Bell Pepper, Chopped
2 C	Diced Cooked Chicken
4	Green Onions, Chopped
¼ tsp	Chopped Pimiento
⅓ C + 1 T	Flour
⅛ tsp	Pepper

DIRECTIONS

1. In large skillet, melt margarine and sauté mushrooms, green pepper and green onions until tender.
2. Blend in flour and pepper and stir until vegetables are coated.
3. Remove from heat and slowly stir in broth and evaporated skimmed milk.
4. Return to heat and bring to a boil, stirring constantly. Boil for 1 minute.
5. Add chicken and pimiento continuing to stir until chicken is heated through.

Yield: *4-6 Servings*
Per Serving: *Calories 195; Fat 5.1 g*

Turkey Jambalaya

INGREDIENTS

1 Lb	Turkey Sausage
1½ Lb (4 C)	Cooked, Diced Turkey Breast Or Thighs
2	Large Onions, Chopped
2 pkg	(6 oz) Long Grain and Wild Rice Mix
1 can	(2½ oz) Sliced Black Olives
1 can	(14½ oz) Artichoke Hearts, Quartered
½ C	Chopped Green Onions
2 T	Light Margarine
1 Lb	Fresh Mushrooms, Sliced

DIRECTIONS

1. In large pot, cut sausage into pieces and brown. Add onions cooking until tender. Drain off any excess grease.
2. Add wild rice to sausage and cook according to directions on package omitting margarine.
3. In another pan, sauté mushrooms in margarine. Drain.
4. Add mushrooms, turkey, black olives, and artichoke hearts to cooked rice, tossing gently.
5. Top with chopped green onions. Bake at 350 degrees for 30 minutes or until thoroughly heated.

Yield: *8-10 Servings*
Per Serving: *Calories 343; Fat 10.2 g*

Lemon Herb Turkey Cutlets

INGREDIENTS

½ tsp	Dried Basil
½ tsp	Each: Dried Tarragon, Thyme, Marjoram
¼ tsp	Pepper
¼ tsp	Salt
1¼ Lb	Turkey Breast Cutlets (¼" Thick)
1 T	Olive Oil
3 cloves	Garlic, Minced
1 T	Flour
½ C	Chicken Broth
2 T	Fresh Lemon Juice

DIRECTIONS

1. Combine first six ingredients; sprinkle over both sides of cutlets and set aside.
2. Coat a large skillet with no stick cooking spray; add oil and heat. Add garlic, stirring, in pan. Add cutlets and cook until browned on each side. Remove to platter.
3. Add flour to skillet, stirring all drippings.
4. Gradually add chicken broth and lemon juice stirring until heated and thick.
5. Return cutlets to sauce and serve.

Yield: *4-6 Servings*
Per Serving: *Calories 145; Fat 4*

Mediterranean Style Chicken

INGREDIENTS

1½-2 Lb	Meaty Chicken Pieces (Breasts, Thigh, and Drumsticks)
1 can	(14½ oz) Tomatoes, Cut Up
¼ C	Dry Red Wine
4 oz	Spaghetti, Cooked and Drained
1 tsp	Dried Basil, Crushed
2 tsp	Cornstarch
¼ C	Sliced Pimiento-Stuffed Olives (Optional)
1 tsp	Sugar
1	Bay Leaf
1 T	Water
1 clove	Garlic, Minced

DIRECTIONS

1. Remove skin from chicken; pat chicken dry with paper towels.
2. Spray a 10 inch skillet with nonstick spray coating. Preheat over medium heat.
3. Add chicken and brown for 10 to 15 minutes, turning to brown evenly.
4. Add undrained tomatoes, wine, sugar, basil, garlic, and bay leaf. Bring to boiling; reduce heat. Cover and simmer about 35 minutes or until chicken is

tender.

5. Remove chicken from skillet; keep warm.

6. In a small bowl, stir together water and cornstarch. Stir into tomato mixture in skillet. Cook and stir until thickened and bubbly. Cook and stir for 2 minutes more.

7. Serve chicken and sauce over cooked spaghetti. Garnish with olives, if desired.

Yield: *4 Servings*
Per Serving: *Calories 312; Fat 7 g; Carbs 29 g*

Cheesy Chicken Rolls

INGREDIENTS

½ C	Shredded Low-Fat Mozzarella Cheese
1 jar	(2½ oz) Sliced Mushrooms, Drained
¼ C	Plain Low-Fat Yogurt
1 T	Snipped Chives
1 T	Snipped Parsley
1 T	Chopped Pimento
4	Boneless Skinless Chicken Breast Halves (12 oz Total)
⅛ tsp	Paprika
1 T	Plain Low-Fat Yogurt

DIRECTIONS

1. Preheat oven to 350°.
2. For filling, combine cheese, mushrooms, the ¼ cup yogurt, chives, parsley, and pimento in a small bowl.
3. Place one chicken breast half, boned side up, between two pieces of clear plastic wrap. Working from the center to the edges, pound lightly with a meat mallet to ⅛" thickness. Remove plastic wrap. Repeat with remaining chicken. Sprinkle lightly with salt and pepper.
4. Spread some of the filling on each chicken breast half. Fold in the sides and roll up. Arrange rolls

seam side down in a 2-quart square baking dish.

5. Combine breadcrumbs and paprika. Brush chicken with the 1 tablespoon yogurt; sprinkle with crumb mixture. Bake in a 350° degree oven for 20 to 25 minutes or until chicken is tender and no longer pink.

Yield: *4 Servings*
Per Serving: *Calories 205; Fat 6 g; Carbs 4 g*

Meats

Tasty Taco-Pie

INGREDIENTS

1 Lb	Ground Turkey
2 can	(8 oz) Tomato Sauce
1 pkg	(1.25 oz) Taco Seasoning Mix
1 can	(8 oz) Refrigerated Quick Crescent Dinner Rolls
6 slices	Lite-Line Cheese, Chopped
1 C	Shredded Lettuce
½	Chopped Tomato
¼ C	Jalapeno Peppers, Sliced (Optional)

DIRECTIONS

1. Brown meat, drain.
2. Stir in tomato sauce and seasoning mix, simmer 5 minutes.
3. Press dough onto bottom. And sides of ungreased 12" pizza pan, pressing edges together to form seal. Prick bottom and sides with fork. Bake at 375 degrees for 10 to 12 minutes or until deep golden brown.
4. Fill with meat mixture, cover with chopped lite-line cheese. Continue baking until cheese begins to melt. Top with remaining ingredients.

Yield: *6 Servings*
Per Serving: *Calories 240; Fat 14 g; Carbs 18 g*

Confetti Cheese Omelet

INGREDIENTS

¼ C	Chopped Red Bell Pepper
¼ C	Chopped Green Bell Pepper
¼ C	Sliced Green Onions
1 C	Egg Substitute
¼ tsp	Fresh Ground Pepper
½ C	(2 oz) Shredded Reduced-Fat Sharp Cheddar Cheese

DIRECTIONS

1. Coat a 10-inch nonstick skillet with cooking spray; place over medium heat until hot. Add peppers and onions; cook 4 minutes, stirring occasionally.

2. Pour egg substitute into skillet; sprinkle with salt and pepper. Cook, without stirring, 2 to 3 minutes or until golden brown on bottom. Sprinkle with cheese. Loosen omelet with a spatula; fold in half. Cook 2 minutes or until egg mixture is set and cheese begins to melt.

3. Cut omelet in half. Slide halves onto serving plates.

Yield: 2 Servings
Per Serving: Calories 159; Fat 5.9 g; Carbs 5.3 g

Southwestern Vegetable Bake

INGREDIENTS

2 cans	(11 oz) Whole-Kernel Corn with Sweet Peppers, Drained
1 can	(14.5 oz) Chili-Style Tomatoes, Undrained
1 can	(15.5 oz) White Hominy, Drained
1 can	(15 oz) No-Salt-Added Black Beans, Rinsed and Drained
¼ tsp	Pepper
½ C	(2 oz) Shredded Monterey Jack Cheese with Jalapeno Peppers

DIRECTIONS

1. Preheat oven to 350°.
2. Combine first 5 ingredients in a 2-quart baking dish; stir well. Cover and bake at 350° for 25 minutes or until bubbly. Uncover, sprinkle with cheese and bake 5 minutes.

Yield: *4 Servings*
Per Serving: *Calories 267; Fat 6.0 g; Carbs 49.3 g*

Cheesy Bean Casserole

INGREDIENTS

1 C	Chopped Onion
2 cans	(15 oz) Chile-Hot Kidney Beans, Drained
2 cans	(14.5 oz) No-Salt-Added Whole Tomatoes, Drained and Chopped
½ tsp	Garlic Powder
¼ tsp	Pepper
1 C	(4 oz) Shredded Reduced-Fat Sharp Cheddar Cheese

DIRECTIONS

1. Preheat oven to 400°.

2. Coat a nonstick skillet with cooking spray; place over medium-high heat until hot. Add onion; sauté until tender. Stir in beans and next 3 ingredients. Cook 3 minutes or until thoroughly heated, stirring well.

3. Spoon mixture into 4 individual baking dishes or 1 (8-inch) square baking dish; sprinkle with cheese. Bake, uncovered, at 400° for 5 minutes or until cheese melts. Let stand 5 minutes.

Yield: *4 Servings*
Per Serving: *Calories 274; Fat 6.9 g; Carbs 35.4 g*

Cheesy Quesadillas

INGREDIENTS

4	(8") Fat-Free Flour Tortillas
1 C	(4 oz) Pre-Shredded Reduced-Fat Cheddar Cheese
¼ C	Chopped Green Onions

DIRECTIONS

1. Coat a large nonstick skillet with cooking spray; place over medium-high heat.
2. Place 1 tortilla in skillet, and top with ½ cup cheese, 2 tablespoons onions, and another tortilla.
3. Cook 2 minutes on each side or until lightly browned. Remove from skillet, and keep warm.
4. Repeat with remaining tortillas, cheese, and onions. Cut each quesadilla into 6 wedges.

Yield: *4 Servings (Serving Size: 3 Wedges)*
Per Serving: *Calories 198; Fat 5.6 g; Carbs 25 g*

INGREDIENTS

4	(4 oz) Boneless Center-Cut Pork Loin Chops (½" Thick)
½ tsp	Salt
½ tsp	Coarsely Ground Pepper
⅓ C	Fat-Free, Less-Sodium Chicken Broth
1½ T	Dijon Mustard
⅓ C	Fat-Free Half-and-Half or Evaporated Fat-Free Milk
	Cooking Spray

DIRECTIONS

1. Trim fat from chops. Sprinkle both sides of chops evenly with salt and pepper.
2. Coat a large nonstick skillet with cooking spray; place over medium-high heat until hot. Add chops to skillet and cook 3-4 minutes on each side or until browned. Remove chops from skillet, and keep warm.
3. Add broth to skillet, stirring to loosen browned bits.
4. Combine mustard and half-and-half; add to skillet. Reduce heat, and simmer 7 minutes or until sauce is thickened slightly. Spoon sauce over pork chops.

Yield: *4 Servings*
Per Serving: *Calories 201; Fat 9 g; Carbs 2.7 g*

Glazed Pork Tenderloins

INGREDIENTS

1½ T	Dijon Mustard
1 clove	Clove Garlic, Minced
¼ T	Dried Rosemary
¼ T	Pepper
1 (1 Lb)	Pork Tenderloin
¼ C	Orange Marmalade

DIRECTIONS

1. Combine first 4 ingredients; set aside.
2. Trim fat from tenderloin. Slice tenderloin lengthwise, cutting almost to, but not through, outer edge.
3. Spread mustard mixture in each pocket; press gently to close. Spread orange marmalade over tenderloin.
4. Place tenderloin on rack coated with no stick cooking spray. Place rack in broiler pan; add water to pan. Bake at 325 degrees for 40 45 minutes or until meat thermometer inserted into thickest portion registers 160 degrees. Slice tenderloin.

Yield: *4 Servings*
Per Serving: *Calories 266; Fat 12.7 g*

INGREDIENTS

2 (¾ Lb)	Pork Tenderloins
1 T	Dried Rosemary
2½ T	Dijon Mustard
½ tsp	Dried Thyme
1½ T	Honey
¼ tsp	Pepper

DIRECTIONS

1. Trim fat from tenderloins and place on a rack coated with no stick cooking spray in a shallow roasting pan.

2. In a small bowl, combine remaining ingredients; brush over tenderloins.

3. Insert a meat thermometer into thickest part of tenderloin. Bake at 350 degrees for 50 minutes or until meat thermometer registers 160 degrees, basting frequently with Dijon mustard mixture.

Yield:　　　*4 to 6 Servings*
Per Serving:　*Calories 153; Fat 4.3 g*

INGREDIENTS

2 Lb	Ground Sirloin
1 tsp	Dried Basil
½ tsp	Garlic Powder
½ tsp	Dried Oregano
2 T	Chopped Parsley
1	Egg White
1	Onion, Finely Chopped
	Salt and Pepper to Taste

DIRECTIONS

1. Combine all ingredients together and shape into balls.
2. Broil in oven on baking sheet approximately 10 minutes, turn and broil on other side until done. Drain any grease. Add meatballs to Sauce (see recipe below).

SAUCE

1 jar	Traditional Spaghetti Sauce (26-28 oz)
1 can	(14.5 oz) Whole Tomatoes, Chopped
1 tsp	Dried Oregano
1 tsp	Dried Basil

3. Combine all ingredients in large pan and heat.

Yield: *6 to 8 Servings*
Per Serving: *Calories 227; Fat 6.7 g*

INGREDIENTS

2 Lb	Ground Sirloin
2 C	Chopped Onion
4 cloves	Garlic, Minced
2 cans	(28 oz) Whole Tomatoes, Chopped
1 can	(6 oz) Salt-Free Tomato Paste
⅔ C	Dry Red Wine
1 T	Dried Oregano
1 T	Dried Basil
1 tsp	Dried Thyme
1	Bay Leaf
⅓ C	Chopped Parsley
	Salt and Pepper to Taste

DIRECTIONS

1. Brown ground sirloin, onion, and garlic in pan coated with no stick cooking spray.
2. Add remaining ingredients. Bring to boil; reduce heat, and simmer for 1 hour, stirring occasionally. Serve over pasta.

Yield: *8 to 10 Servings*
Per Serving: *Calories 193; Fat 4.7 g*

Easy Brisket

INGREDIENTS

5-6 Lb	Very Lean Brisket
1 C	Water
	Garlic Powder
1 envelope	Dry Onion Soup Mix
1 C	Light Brown Sugar
1 C	Ketchup

DIRECTIONS

1. Season brisket heavily with garlic powder.
2. Combine remaining ingredients in small bowl. Pour over brisket in baking pan or roaster. Cover and bake at 350 degrees for 4 hours or until tender.

Yield: *12 Servings*
Per Serving: *Calories 386; Fat 13.2 g*

INGREDIENTS

1 (3 Lb)	Lean Beef Brisket
2 C	Water
⅓ **C**	Dijon Mustard
2 tsp	Dried Thyme
½ tsp	Pepper
½ tsp	Salt
4 cloves	Garlic, Minced
1	Onion, Large, Quartered
½ T	Cornstarch

DIRECTIONS

1. Trim all fat from brisket.
2. In a baking pot, add water.
3. In a small bowl, combine mustard, thyme, pepper, salt, and garlic into a paste.
4. Cover brisket with mixture and place in pot. Add carrots and onions around meat. Cover and cook at 325 degrees for 4 hours or until brisket is tender.
5. Slice against grain.

Yield:　　　*6 Servings*
Per Serving:　　*Calories 390; Fat 15.1 g*

Dirty Rice

INGREDIENTS

1 Lb	Extra Lean Ground Beef
2 cloves	Garlic, Minced
1 T	Worcestershire Sauce
2 stalks	Celery, Chopped
¼ tsp	Red Pepper
1 T	Chopped Parsley
¼ tsp	Pepper
1 C	Raw Rice
1	Green Bell Pepper, Seeded, Chopped
1	Red Bell Pepper, Seeded, Chopped
1	Onion, Chopped
1 can	(14.5 oz) Beef Broth
1 C	Water

DIRECTIONS

1. In large skillet, add beef and all vegetables cooking until beef is done and vegetables are tender.
2. Add seasonings, stirring well.
3. Add rice, broth, and water, mixing well. Bring to a boil and reduce heat, cover, and cook for 25 to 30 minutes or until rice is done.

Yield: *4 to 6 Servings*
Per Serving: *Calories 313; Fat 13.4 g*

Barbecue Pork Chops

INGREDIENTS

8 (5 oz)	Bone-In Center-Cut Pork Chops (½")
¼ tsp	Pepper
½ C	Thick-and-Spicy Honey Barbecue Sauce
1 can	(14.5 oz) No-Salt-Added Stewed Tomatoes, Undrained
1 pkg	(10 oz) Frozen Vegetable Seasoning Blend
	Cooking Spray

DIRECTIONS

1. Trim fat from chops; sprinkle chops with pepper.
2. Coat a large nonstick skillet with cooking spray; place over medium-high heat until hot. Add chops, in two batches, and cook until browned on both sides.
3. Coat a 3½ or 4 quart electric slow cooker with cooking spray. Place chops on cooker.
4. Combine barbecue sauce, tomatoes, and frozen vegetable blend, stirring well; pour mixture over chops.
5. Cover and cook on high-heat setting 4 hours. Or, cover and cook on high-heat setting 1 hour; reduce to low-heat setting, and cook 7 hours.

Yield:　　　*8 Servings*
Per Serving:　　*Calories 237; Fat 8.2 g; Carbs 12.4 g*

INGREDIENTS

4 (6 oz)	Bone-In Center-Cut Pork Chops (½")
	Cooking Spray
1½ C	Quick-Cooking 5-Minute Rice, Uncooked
⅔ C	Water
½ C	Chopped Onion
¼ tsp	Pepper
1 can	(14.5 oz) Italian-Style Stewed Tomatoes, Undrained and Chopped
1 can	(8 oz) No-Salt-Added Tomato Sauce

DIRECTIONS

1. Trim fat from chops.
2. Coat a large nonstick skillet with cooking spray, and place over medium-high heat until hot. Add chops, and cook 2 minutes on each side. Remove from skillet; set aside.
3. Combine rice and remaining 5 ingredients in skillet; bring to a boil.
4. Arrange chops over rice mixture. Cover, reduce heat, and cook 5 minutes or until liquid is absorbed and rice is done.

Yield: *4 Servings*
Per Serving: *Calories 375; Fat 8.5 g; Carbs 42.9 g*

Italian Pot Roast

INGREDIENTS

1 (2½ Lb)	Boneless Round Roast
1	Medium Onion
¼ tsp	Salt
¼ tsp	Pepper
2 cans	(8 oz) No-Salt-Added Tomato Sauce
1 pkg	(.7 oz) Italian Salad Dressing Mix

DIRECTIONS

1. Slice roast in half for even cooking; place in a 3 1/2 quart electric slow cooker.
2. Add onion and remaining ingredients. Cover and cook on high heat setting 5 hours or until roast is tender. Or, cover and cook on high heat setting 1 hour; reduce to low heat setting, and cook 7 hours. Slice meat to serve.

Yield: *8 Servings*
Per Serving: *Calories 223; Fat 5.8 g; Carbs 7.4 g*

Chef Bailey's Cherished Recipes Made Healthier

Barbecue Meat Loaf

INGREDIENTS

1 Lb	Ground Round
½ C	Barbecue Sauce, Divided
¼ C	Frozen Chopped Onion, Pressed Dry
¼ C	Italian Seasoned Dry Breadcrumbs
2	Large Egg Whites
¼ tsp	Pepper

DIRECTIONS

1. Preheat oven to 375 degrees.
2. Combine meat, ¼ cup barbecue sauce, onion, breadcrumbs, egg whites, and pepper in a large bowl; stir well.
3. Shape mixture into a 7 x 5 inch loaf on a rack in a roasting pan.
4. Spread remaining ¼ barbecue sauce over loaf. Bake at 375 degrees for 25 minutes or to desired degree of doneness.

Yield: *4 Servings*
Per Serving: *Calories 228; Fat 7.6 g; Carbs 10.4 g*

Fish & Shellfish

Ground Beef Stroganoff

INGREDIENTS

8 oz	Wide Egg Noodles, Uncooked
1 Lb	Ground Round
3	Green Onions, Sliced (or 1 Cup Chopped Onion)
1 pkg	(8 oz) Pre-Sliced Mushrooms
1 jar	(12 oz) Fat-Free Beef Gravy
1 carton	(8 oz) Fat-Free Sour Cream
¼ tsp	Garlic Salt
¼ tsp	Freshly Ground Pepper
1 T	Dry Sherry (Optional)

DIRECTIONS

1. Prepare noodles according to package directions, omitting salt and fat.
2. While noodles cook, cook meat, green onions, and mushrooms in a large nonstick skillet until meat is browned, stirring until it crumbles; drain.
3. Return meat mixture to skillet; add gravy and next 3 ingredients, stirring well. Cook over medium heat 3 to 5 minutes or until thoroughly heated. Stir in sherry, if desired. Serve over drained noodles.

Yield: *5 Servings*
Per Serving: *Calories 367; Fat 7.6 g; Carbs 42.9 g*

Deep-Dish Pizza Casserole

INGREDIENTS

1 Lb	Ground Round
1 can	(15 oz) Chunky Italian-Style Tomato Sauce
	Cooking Spray
1 can	(10 oz) Refrigerated Pizza Crust Dough
1½ C	(6 oz) Pre-Shredded Part Skim Mozzarella Cheese

DIRECTIONS

1. Preheat oven to 425 degrees.
2. Cook meat in a nonstick skillet over medium high heat until browned, stirring until it crumbles. Drain, if necessary, and return to skillet. Add tomato sauce, and cook until heated.
3. While meat cooks, coat a 13 x 9 inch baking dish with cooking spray.
4. Unroll pizza crust dough, and press into bottom and halfway up sides of baking dish. Top bottom of pizza crust with meat mixture. Bake, uncovered, at 425 degrees for 12 minutes.
5. Top with cheese, and bake 5 minutes or until crust is browned and cheese melts. Cool 5 minutes before serving.

Yield: *6 Servings*
Per Serving: *Calories 277; Fat 7.7 g; Carbs 28.5 g*

Tex-Mex Pepper Steak

INGREDIENTS

2	Regular Sized Bags Boil-In-Bag Rice
¾ Lb	Flank Steak
1 pkg	(16 oz) Frozen Pepper Stir Fry
1 can	(14.5 oz) Mexican-Style Tomatoes, Undrained
	Cooking Spray
¼ tsp	Salt
1 tsp	Ground Cumin
2 T	Chili Powder

DIRECTIONS

1. Prepare rice according to package directions, omitting salt and fat, to make 4 cups cooked rice.

2. While rice cooks, slice steak in half lengthwise; slice each half diagonally across grain into ¼ inch thick slices.

3. Combine chili powder, cumin, and salt in a zip-top plastic bag; add meat. Seal bag, and shake until meat is well coated.

4. Coat a large nonstick skillet with cooking spray; place over medium high heat until hot. Add meat; stir-fry 4 minutes or until browned. Remove meat from skillet, and set aside; wipe drippings from skillet with a paper towel.

5. Coat skillet with cooking spray; place over medium heat until hot. Add pepper stir-fry; stir-fry 2 minutes or just until tender. Add tomatoes; bring to a boil. Cook 2 minutes, stirring occasionally.

6. Return meat to skillet; cook until thoroughly heated. Remove skillet from heat. Place 1 cup rice on each of 4 plates; top evenly with meat mixture.

Yield: 4 Servings
Per Serving: Calories 437; Fat 10.9 g; Carbs 61.6 g

INGREDIENTS

8 oz	Bow Tie Pasta, Uncooked
1 Lb	Fresh Asparagus
1 C	Frozen English Peas
¼ C	Sliced Green Onions
½ tsp	Freshly Ground Pepper
2 cans	(6 oz) Low-Sodium White Tuna Packed in Water, Drained And Coarsely Flaked
2 T	Olive Oil
1 C	Chopped Seeded Tomato
¼ C	Lemon Juice
½ tsp	Salt

DIRECTIONS

1. Cook pasta according to package directions, omitting salt and fat; drain, reserving 3 tablespoons of pasta water.

2. While pasta cooks, snap off tough ends of asparagus. Cut asparagus into 1-inch pieces. Combine asparagus and peas in a steamer basket over boiling water. Cover and steam 3 to 4 minutes or until asparagus is crisp-tender. Drain.

3. Combine steamed vegetables, green onions, salt, and olive oil in a large bowl.

4. Add pasta, reserved pasta water, tomato, and

lemon juice; toss well. Add tuna; toss. Sprinkle with freshly ground pepper.

Yield: 6 Servings
Per Serving: Calories 249; Fat 3.8 g; Carbs 36 g

Crab Cakes

INGREDIENTS

1 Lb	Lump Crabmeat
¼ tsp	Pepper
1 can	(8 oz) Water Chestnuts, Drained and Finely Chopped
Dash	Hot Sauce
1	Egg White, Slightly Beaten
3 T	Fat Free Mayonnaise
2	Green Onions, Chopped
¼ C	Soft Bread Crumbs
1 T	Finely Chopped Parsley

DIRECTIONS

1. Combine all ingredients gently together.
2. Shape into 8 patties.
3. Coat a skillet with no stick cooking spray; heat until hot. Add crab patties and cook until lightly browned on both sides, turning once.

Yield: *4 Servings*
Per Serving: *Calories 179; Fat 2.4 g*

INGREDIENTS

4 T	Light Margarine
5 T	Olive Oil
½ C	Free Italian Dressing
6 cloves	Garlic, Minced
1 tsp	Hot Pepper Sauce
¼ C	Worcestershire Sauce
1 tsp	Dried Oregano
1 tsp	Dried Rosemary
1 tsp	Dried Thyme
1 tsp	Pepper
1 tsp	Salt, If Desired
2 tsp	Paprika
8	Bay Leaves
2 Lb	Headless Shrimp (Unpeeled)
2 oz	Dry White Wine

DIRECTIONS

1. In large heavy skillet, melt margarine, then add oil and mix well.
2. Add all the other ingredients, except for shrimp and wine, and cook over medium heat until sauce begins to boil.
3. Add the shrimp and cook approximately 15

minutes.

4. Add wine and cook another 10 minutes or until shrimp are done. Serve shrimp with sauce.

Yield: 4 to 6 Servings
Per Serving: Calories 328; Fat 17.7 g

Baked Trout with Lemon Sauce

INGREDIENTS

2 Lb	Trout Fillets (or Fish of Your Choice)
1 T	Finely Chopped Parsley
	Salt and Pepper to Taste
4	Green Onions, Chopped
	Paprika

DIRECTIONS

1. Place fillets on baking sheet lined with foil.
2. Sprinkle with salt, pepper, green onions, and parsley. Then sprinkle with paprika.
3. Cover with lemon sauce (see recipe below). Bake at 375 degrees for 25 minutes, baste with lemon sauce during cooking.

LEMON SAUCE

¼ C	Light Margarine, Melted
2 T	Lemon Juice
2 cloves	Garlic, Minced

4. Combine all ingredients and pour over prepared fish.

Yield: *6 Servings*
Per Serving: *Calories 159; Fat 5 g*

INGREDIENTS

3 T	Light Margarine
½ C	White Wine
4 cloves	(Large) Garlic, Minced
3 T	Green Onion, Chopped
	Salt and Pepper to Taste
2 T	Finely Chopped Parsley
2-3 Lb	Trout Fillets

DIRECTIONS

1. Melt margarine in large skillet coated with no stick cooking spray.
2. Add garlic and sauté for several minutes.
3. Season fillets with salt and pepper. Add fillets, cooking until almost done.
4. Add white wine and turn fish.
5. Sprinkle with green onions and parsley; continue cooking until fish is flaky.

Yield: *6 Servings*
Per Serving: *Calories 266; Fat 9.3 g*

Country Catfish

INGREDIENTS

	Butter Flavored Cooking Spray
⅔ C	Corn Flake Crumbs
¼ tsp	Salt
¼ tsp	Ground Red Pepper
4	(6 oz) Farm-Raised Catfish Fillets
2	Egg Whites, Lightly Beaten
¼ C	Commercial Corn Relish

DIRECTIONS

1. Preheat oven to 450 degrees.
2. Line a shallow pan with aluminum foil. Coat with cooking spray.
3. Combine crumbs, salt, and pepper in a small bowl; stir well.
4. Dip fish in beaten egg whites; dredge in crumb mixture.
5. Place fish in pan. Bake at 450 degrees for 8 to 10 minutes or until fish flakes easily when tested with a fork. Serve immediately with corn relish.

Yield: 4 Servings (Serving Size: 1 fillet and 2 T relish)
Per Serving: Calories 250; Fat 5 g; Carbs 18.7 g

Baked Catfish

INGREDIENTS

1 Lb	Catfish Fillets
2 tsp	Powdered Rosemary
½ tsp	Black Pepper
2	Lemons, Peeled and Finely Chopped
¼ C	Chopped Fresh Parsley
	Olive Oil Vegetable Spray

DIRECTIONS

1. Spray pan and fish with nonstick olive oil spray.

2. Sprinkle fish generously with powdered rosemary and black pepper. Arrange in baking dish. Bake 325 degrees 15-20 minutes or until fish flakes easily when tested with a fork.

3. Remove to serving plate. Cover with lemons. Sprinkle with parsley.

Yield: *4 Servings*
Per Serving: *Calories 184; Fat 4 g; Carbs 17 g*

Pasta & Bread

Grilled Catfish

INGREDIENTS

1 Lb	Catfish Fillets
½ C	Oil Free Italian Dressing

DIRECTIONS

1. Marinate fish for 30 minutes to one hour before cooking in diet Italian dressing.
2. Prepare coals. Cover the grill with foil or use a fish basket.
3. Grill 5-6 minutes. Turn, grill 3-5 minutes or until fish flakes easily when tested with a fork.

Yield: *4 Servings*
Per Serving: *Calories 168; Fat 4 g; Carbs 13*

Crawfish Jambalaya

INGREDIENTS

1	Large Yellow Onion, Chopped
1 clove	(Large) Garlic, Minced
1	Large Green Pepper, Chopped
1 tsp	Tabasco Pepper Sauce
1	Celery Rib, Diced with Tops
1 can	(18 oz) Tomatoes
¼ C	Tomato Sauce
½ tsp	Dried Leaf Thyme
2	Large Bay Leaves
1½ Lb	Fresh Crawfish
2 C	Rice, Uncooked
¼ C	Oil
2 T	Minced Parsley

DIRECTIONS

1. Sauté onion, garlic, green pepper, and celery in oil (moderate heat) until onion is golden.
2. Add parsley, thyme, and bay leaves. Cook 5 minutes, stirring often.
3. Add Tabasco, tomatoes (and juice), tomato sauce, 2 cups water, and 2 teaspoons salt. Simmer 5 minutes.
4. Add rice, reduce heat to simmer and cook covered

30 minutes.

5. Add crawfish and simmer covered 10 to 15 minutes until rice is tender and all liquid is absorbed. Season to taste with Tabasco.

Yield: *8 Servings*
Per Serving: *Calories 301 Fat 9 g; Carbs 23 g*

Jumbo Stuffed Shells

INGREDIENTS

1 pkg	(12 oz) Jumbo Shells
1½ Lb	Ground Sirloin
2	Egg Whites
¼ C	Grated Parmesan Cheese
1 pkg	(8 oz) Part-Skim Mozzarella Cheese, Shredded
1 T	Chopped Parsley
1 tsp	Dried Basil
½ tsp	Oregano
	Salt and Pepper to Taste
¼ C	Breadcrumbs

DIRECTIONS

1. Cook pasta shells according to directions on package omitting oil; drain and set aside.
2. In skillet, cook sirloin until done. Drain any excess fat. Combine with remaining ingredients except cheese. Stuff shells with filling.
3. Pour half the Tomato Sauce (see recipe below) in a 2-quart baking dish. Arrange stuffed shells on top and cover with remaining sauce. Bake at 350 degrees for 20 minutes.
4. Sprinkle with mozzarella cheese and continue baking for 10 minutes longer.

TOMATO SAUCE

1 T	Olive Oil
1	Medium Onion, Chopped
½ tsp	Sugar
3 C	Tomato Juice
1 can	(6 oz) Tomato Paste
2 cloves	Garlic, Minced
	Salt and Pepper to Taste

5. In skillet, sauté onion in olive oil until tender. Add remaining ingredients; simmer 10 minutes.

Yield: *6 to 8 Servings*
Per Serving: *Calories 425; Fat 12 g*

INGREDIENTS

1 pkg	(12 oz) Linguine
1½ Lb	Skinless, Boneless Chicken Pieces
¼ C	Olive Oil
3 cloves	Garlic, Minced
½ Lb	Mushrooms, Sliced
¼ C	Grated Parmesan Cheese
1	Red Bell Pepper, Chopped
1 C	Frozen Peas
½ tsp	Dried Oregano
½ tsp	Dried Basil
½ tsp	Dried Thyme
1	Onion, Chopped
	Salt and Pepper to Taste

DIRECTIONS

1. Cook linguine according to directions on package; drain.
2. In large frying pan, cook chicken pieces in olive oil and garlic until lightly brown and done. Watch carefully, tossing to keep from sticking.
3. Add mushrooms, onions, red pepper, and seasonings, sautéing until tender. Add peas, tossing until heated.

4. When pasta is ready, add to vegetable mixture, combining well. Add Parmesan cheese and serve.

Yield: *6 to 8 Servings*
Per Serving: *Calories 365; Fat 9.7 g*

INGREDIENTS

1 Lb	Skinless, Boneless Chicken Breasts, Cut Into Bitesized Pieces
2 cloves	(Large) Garlic, Minced
2 C	Thinly Sliced Zucchini
½ C	Chopped Onion
4 C	Cooked Fettuccine
½ tsp	Dried Basil
1 can	(5⅓ oz) Evaporated Skimmed Milk
	Salt and Pepper as Desired

DIRECTIONS

1. Coat a large pot with no stick cooking spray and sauté chicken, onion, basil, salt and pepper, and garlic until chicken is almost done.
2. Add zucchini, sauté until tender.
3. Cook fettuccine according to directions on package omitting oil; drain.
4. Remove pan with chicken from heat and add fettuccine and milk, tossing gently.

Yield: *4 Servings*
Per Serving: *Calories 391; Fat 4 g*

Chicken and Linguine

INGREDIENTS

2 T	Margarine
1	Medium Onion, Thinly Sliced in Rings
2 cloves	Garlic, Minced
1 tsp	Dried Basil
¼ tsp	Crushed Red Pepper
1½ Lb	Chicken Breasts, Cut in Pieces
8 oz	Linguine
¼ C	Freshly Grated Parmesan Cheese
	Salt and Pepper, if Desired

DIRECTIONS

1. Melt margarine in a 13 x9x2 inch baking dish in a preheated 400 degree oven.
2. Remove pan from oven and stir in onion, garlic, basil and red pepper.
3. Roll chicken pieces in margarine mixture and leave in pan. Return pan to oven and bake chicken, uncovered, about 45 minutes.
4. Approximately 10 minutes before chicken is done, cook linguine according to package directions without oil. Drain.
5. When chicken is done, add pasta, cheese, salt, and pepper to dish, mixing well.

Yield: *4 Servings*
Per Serving: *Calories 468; Fat 11.4 g*

Shrimp Fettuccine

INGREDIENTS

1 Lb	Large Shrimp, Peeled
¼ C	White Wine
1 pkg	(8 oz) Fettuccine
1 bunch	Green Onions, Finely Chopped
4 T	Finely Chopped Parsley
3 T	Light Margarine
2 cloves	Garlic, Minced
½ Lb	Mushrooms, Sliced
½ C	Finely Grated Romano Cheese
1 pkg	(6 oz) Frozen Snow Peas

DIRECTIONS

1. Marinate shrimp in white wine for 1 hour.
2. In large skillet, stir fry onions, garlic, mushrooms, and snow peas in margarine.
3. When vegetables are crisp tender, add shrimp and sauté until shrimp are pink.
4. Meanwhile, prepare fettuccine according to directions on package omitting oil. Drain.
5. Add fettuccine to shrimp mixture with parsley and Romano cheese, tossing gently.

Yield: *6 to 8 Servings*
Per Serving: *Calories 208; Fat 5.7 g*

INGREDIENTS

1 Lb	Uncooked Shrimp, Peeled
⅛ tsp	Red Pepper
8	Zucchini, Thinly Sliced
8 oz	Ziti Pasta
1	Carrot, Peeled and Shredded
½ C	Evaporated Skimmed Milk
½ C	Finely Chopped Green Onions
⅔ C	Low Fat 1% Cottage Cheese, Pureed

DIRECTIONS

1. Coat a skillet with no stick cooking spray, and add the shrimp, zucchini, carrots, green onions, and red pepper. Cook, stirring, until the shrimp are done, turning pink.

2. Cook pasta according to directions on package omitting oil; drain.

3. Stir cooked pasta into vegetable mixture, tossing until well mixed. Remove from skillet and transfer to dish.

4. In same skillet, add milk and cottage cheese; bring to a boil. Cook, stirring, until the sauce thickens.

5. Return shrimp pasta mixture to skillet cooking until thoroughly heated.

Yield: *4 to 6 Servings*
Per Serving: *Calories 258; Fat 2.1 g*

INGREDIENTS

12 oz	Angel Hair Pasta
3 T	Olive Oil
2 cloves	Garlic, Minced
1 T	Finely Chopped Parsley

DIRECTIONS

1. Cook pasta according to directions on package, omitting salt and oil.
2. Drain and set aside.
3. In a small pan, combine all remaining ingredients and sauté for a few minutes.
4. Pour over cooked pasta and toss. Serve immediately.

Yield: *6 to 8 Servings*
Per Serving: *Calories 215; Fat 5.9 g*

Low Fat Broccoli Lasagna

INGREDIENTS

1	Green Bell Pepper, Seeded and Chopped
1½ C	Low-Fat Cottage Cheese
2 cloves	Garlic, Chopped
1 T	Skim Milk
1 tsp	Dried Oregano
1 C	Shredded Part-Skim Mozzarella Cheese
2 T	Grated Parmesan Cheese
2 pkg	(10 oz) Frozen Chopped Broccoli, Thawed and Rained
1	Egg White
1	Onion, Chopped
2 T	Flour
5	Lasagna Noodles
½ tsp	Dried Basil
¾ C	Skim Milk
	Salt and Pepper to Taste

DIRECTIONS

1. Coat a large skillet with no stick cooking spray. Heat and add green pepper, onion, and garlic. Sauté until tender. Add flour, oregano, basil, and salt and pepper to taste. Cook 1 minute, stirring constantly. Gradually add ¾ cup milk, stirring constantly. Cook,

stirring, until mixture is thickened. Stir in broccoli; set aside.

2. Combine cottage cheese, egg white, and 1 tablespoon milk in food processor until smooth.

3. Coat a 9-inch square baking pan with no stick cooking spray.

4. Spoon ⅓ broccoli mixture into dish. Break noodles in half crosswise. Place 4 noodle halves over broccoli mixture. Spread half of cottage cheese mixture over noodles; top with mozzarella cheese. Repeat layers, ending with broccoli mixture.

5. Cover and refrigerate at least 8 hours. Sprinkle with Parmesan cheese. Bake, uncovered, at 375 degrees for 40 minutes or until bubbly. Let stand 10 minutes before cutting.

Yield: *6 to 8 Servings*
Per Serving: *Calories 187; Fat 4.3 g*

INGREDIENTS

½ Lb	Fresh Mushrooms, Cut in Half
1 bunch	Broccoli, Flowerets Only
1	Red Bell Pepper, Cut into Strips
1 pkg	(12 oz) Tri-Colored Pasta Shells
1 pkg	(6 oz) Tri-Colored Stuffed Tortellini
2 C	Snow Peas
⅓ C	Grated Romano Cheese
1 C	Cherry Tomatoes, Cut in Half

DIRECTIONS

1. Cook snow peas and broccoli in microwave until crisp tender. Drain and set aside.
2. Cook pasta shells and tortellini according to directions on package omitting salt and oil. Drain and set aside.
3. Combine all ingredients in large bowl. Toss with Dressing. (See recipe below.)

DRESSING

1 bunch	Green Onions, Sliced
½ C	Red Wine Vinegar
⅓ C	Olive Oil
2 T	Chopped Parsley

2 tsp	Dried Basil
3 cloves	Garlic, Minced
1½ tsp	Dijon Mustard
1 tsp	Dried Dill Weed
½ tsp	Dried Oregano
1 tsp	Salt
½ tsp	Sugar
½ tsp	Pepper

Yield: *10 Servings*
Per Serving: *Calories 324; Fat 9.4 g*

Chef Bailey's Cherished Recipes Made Healthier

Biscuits

INGREDIENTS

1 C	Flour
1½ tsp	Baking Powder
⅛ tsp	Baking Soda
⅛ tsp	Salt
2 T	Light Margarine
½ C	No Fat Plain Yogurt
1 tsp	Honey

DIRECTIONS

1. Combine flour, baking powder, baking soda, and salt in bowl; cut in margarine with pastry blender or fork until mixture resembles coarse meal.

2. Add yogurt and honey, stirring just until dry ingredients are moistened.

3. Turn dough onto floured surface and knead 4 times.

4. Roll dough to ½-inch thickness; cut with cutter about 1½-inches wide.

5. Place on un-greased baking sheet. Bake at 425 degrees for 10 minutes or until golden. Serve hot.

Yield: *8 Servings*
Per Serving: *Calories 81; Fat 1.5 g*

Blueberry Bread

INGREDIENTS

2 C	Flour
¼ C	Hot Water
1 C	Sugar
½ C	Orange Juice
1 tsp	Baking Powder
1 T	Grated Orange Rind
¼ T	Salt
¼ tsp	Baking Soda
1	Egg, Beaten
2 T	Light Margarine, Melted
1 C	Blueberries

DIRECTIONS

1. Combine all dry ingredients in bowl.
2. In another bowl, mix melted margarine, hot water, orange juice, orange rind, and egg.
3. Fold dry ingredients into orange juice mixture. Fold in blueberries.
4. Pour batter into a 9x5x3-inch loaf pan coated with no stick cooking spray and dusted with flour. Bake at 350 degrees for 50 to 60 minutes. Remove bread from pan and spread with Glaze (see recipe below).

GLAZE

2 T	Orange Juice
½ tsp	Grated Orange Rind
2 T	Honey

5. Bring all ingredients to a boil in a saucepan and boil for 1 minute or bring to boil in microwave. Spread over bread.

Yield: *16 Slices*
Per Serving: *Calories 139; Fat 1.2 g*

Banana Raisin Bread

INGREDIENTS

1½ C	Flour
2	Eggs
1 tsp	Baking Soda
1 tsp	Vanilla
1 C	Sugar
½ C	Safflower Oil
½ tsp	Salt
¾ C	Non-Fat Plain Yogurt
3-4	Bananas, Mashed (About 1½ Cups)
⅔ C	Raisins

DIRECTIONS

1. In bowl, combine all dry ingredients.
2. In another bowl, whisk together bananas, eggs, vanilla, and oil. Fold yogurt into banana mixture. Add raisins.
3. Pour banana raisin mixture over dry ingredients and pour batter into a 9x5x3-inch loaf pan coated with no stick cooking spray and dusted with flour. Bake at 350 degrees for 50 to 60 minutes. Cool in pan.

Yield: *16 Slices*
Per Serving: *Calories 202; Fat 7.7 g*

Banana Bread

INGREDIENTS

½ C	Light Margarine
1 T	Baking Powder
⅓ C	Sugar
1 tsp	Baking Soda
½ C	Light Brown Sugar
1 tsp	Cinnamon
3	Medium Bananas, Mashed
½ C	Chopped Pecans, Toasted
1 tsp	Vanilla
4	Egg Whites, Beaten until Frothy
2 tsp	Lemon Juice
2 C	Flour

DIRECTIONS

1. In mixing bowl, cream margarine and sugars.
2. Stir in bananas, vanilla, and lemon juice,
3. Combine flour with baking powder, baking soda, and cinnamon; add to banana mixture. Stir in pecans.
4. Fold in egg whites and pour into a 9x5x3-inch pan coated with no stick cooking spray and dusted with flour. Bake at 350 degrees for 45 to 50 minutes or until done.

Yield: *16 Servings*
Per Serving: *Calories 176; Fat 5.4 g*

Sweet Potato Rolls

INGREDIENTS

1 C	Cooked Mashed Sweet Potatoes (About 1 Large)
1½ C	Warm Water
1	Egg
3 T	Light Margarine, Melted
1 tsp	Salt
1 pkg	Rapid Rise Yeast
3 T	Sugar
5 C	Flour

DIRECTIONS

1. Blend potatoes with melted margarine.
2. Dissolve yeast in ½ cup warm water.
3. Combine potatoes with egg, salt, sugar, and yeast mixture. Add flour alternately with remaining ¾ cup warm water, mixing until well combined.
4. Turn onto a well-floured board and knead. Place in bowl coated with no stick cooking spray; cover.
5. Allow to rise for 1 hour in warm place.
6. Remove to board and roll to one-inch thickness and cut into round circles with cutter or glass.
7. Place on baking sheet coated with cooking spray and let rise in warm place for 30 minutes or until doubled in size. Bake at 425 degrees for 15-20 minutes.

Yield: *24 Rolls*
Per Serving: *Calories 129; Fat 1.2 g*

Corn Bread

INGREDIENTS

2 C	White Cornmeal
1 C	Flour
½ C	Sugar
1 tsp	Baking Soda
2 C	Low Fat Buttermilk
3 T	Canola Oil

DIRECTIONS

1. Combine dry ingredients.
2. Mix buttermilk and oil; stir into dry mixture. Mix well.
3. Pour batter into a 9x5x3-ineh loaf pan coated with no stick cooking spray and dusted with flour. Bake at 350 degrees for 55 minutes. Serve hot.

Yield: *16 Servings*
Per Serving: *Calories 129; Fat 3.1 g*

Garlic Bread

INGREDIENTS

1 Loaf   (6 oz) French Bread
              Olive Oil-Flavored Cooking Spray
1 T   Minced Garlic

DIRECTIONS

1. Preheat oven to 350°.
2. Slice loaf into 4 slices, and coat each slice with cooking spray. Spread garlic evenly over slices. Wrap loaf in aluminum foil, and bake at 350° for 10 minutes or until thoroughly heated.

Yield: *4 Slices*
Per Slice: *Calories 129; Fat 1.1 g; Carbs 24.3 g*

Garlic-Cheese Breadsticks

INGREDIENTS

¼ C	(1 oz) Grated Parmesan Cheese
¼ C	Garlic Powder
1 can	(11 oz) Refrigerated Soft Breadstick Dough

DIRECTIONS

1. Combine cheese and garlic powder. Prepare breadsticks according to package directions, pressing each stick into cheese mixture before baking.

Yield: *8 breadsticks*
Per Breadstick: Calories 122; Fat 2.8 g; Carbs 19.2 g

Quick Corn Bread

INGREDIENTS

1 pkg   (7.5 oz) Yellow Corn Muffin Mix

2 C   Water

        Cooking Spray

DIRECTIONS

1. Preheat oven to 400°.
2. Prepare muffin mix according to package directions using 2 cups water. Pour batter into an 8-inch ovenproof skillet coated with cooking spray, and bake at 400° for 16 minutes or until golden. Cut into wedges.

Yield: *6 Wedges*
Per Wedge: *Calories 133; Fat 2.9 g; Carbs 25.8 g*

Banana Muffins

INGREDIENTS

⅓ C	All-Purpose Flour
1 C	Whole Wheat Flour
⅓ C	Granulated Sugar
1 T	Baking Powder
2 tsp	Baking Soda
2 tsp	Cinnamon
2 tsp	Nutmeg
2 C	Low-Fat Buttermilk
⅓ C	Vegetable Oil
1	Ripe Banana (Mashed)
1	Egg

DIRECTIONS

1. In mixing bowl, combine all dry ingredients.
2. In separate small bowl, combine remaining ingredients.
3. Mix dry with moist ingredients stirring until all ingredients are moist.
4. Fill paper-lined muffin tins or spray tins with nonstick vegetable spray filling : full. — THE QUANTITY IS MISSING
5. Bake at 375° for 15-20 minutes.

Yield: *18 Muffins*
Per Muffin: *Calories 105; Fat 1 g; Carbs 22 g*

INGREDIENTS

2 C	All-Purpose Flour
4 tsp	Baking Powder
2 tsp	Salt
1 T	Sugar
6 T	Margarine
1 C	2% Milk

DIRECTIONS

1. Mix together first 4 ingredients.
2. Add margarine and cut until about consistency of corn meal.
3. Add milk in with fork.
4. On floured cutting board, knead gently, turning over several times. Roll with dusted rolling pin to 2" thickness.
5. Cut to desired size with a glass.
6. Bake with sides touching on ungreased cookie sheet on high shelf in oven at 450° for about 10-12 minutes.

Yield: *16 Biscuits*
Per Biscuit: *Calories 96; Fat 1 g; Carbs 14 g*

Chef Bailey's Cherished Recipes Made Healthier

INGREDIENTS

¼ C	Vegetable Oil
¾ C	Brown Sugar
2 C	All-Purpose Flour
3 tsp	Baking Powder
3 tsp	Salt
1 C	Low-Fat Buttermilk
3 C	Eggbeaters
1 tsp	Baking Soda
⅓ C	Oat Bran
1 C	Raisins

DIRECTIONS

1. In a mixing bowl, combine all dry ingredients.
2. In separate small bowl, combine remaining ingredients.
3. Mix dry with moist ingredients stirring until all ingredients are moist.
4. Fill paper-lined muffin tins or spray tins with nonstick vegetable spray.
5. Fill tins: full. Bake at 400° for 15-20 minutes.

Yield: *18 Muffins*
Per Muffin: *Calories 119; Fat 3 g; Carbs 21 g*

Chili Corn Bread Pie

INGREDIENTS

1	Onion, Chopped
1 C	(4 oz) Pre-Shredded Reduced Fat Mexican Blend or Cheddar Cheese
1 can	(15 oz) Low-Fat Chili Beef Soup
1 can	(11 oz) Mexican-Style Corn, Drained
1 pkg	(6 oz) Buttermilk Corn Bread Mix
⅔ C	Water

DIRECTIONS

1. Preheat oven to 450 degrees.

2. Coat a nonstick skillet with cooking spray; place over medium high heat until hot. Add onion, and sauté until tender.

3. Add soup and corn to skillet, stirring well; spoon mixture into an 8 inch square baking dish coated with cooking spray. Sprinkle cheese over soup mixture.

4. Combine corn bread mix and water, stirring just until smooth. Pour batter over mixture in baking dish; bake at 450 degrees for 18 minutes or until golden.

Yield: *6 Servings*
Per Serving: *Calories 270; Fat 7.3 g; Carbs 39.5 g*

Salads

Romaine & Tomato Salad

INGREDIENTS

4 C	Shredded Romaine Lettuce
12	Cherry Tomatoes, Halved
1	Red Onion, Sliced
½ C	Fat-Free French Dressing

DIRECTIONS

1. Combine lettuce, tomato, and onion.
2. Drizzle with dressing; toss.

Yield: *4 (1¼-Cup) Servings*
Per Serving: *Calories 81 Fat 0.3 g; Carbs 18.3 g*

Tossed Salad with Feta

INGREDIENTS

4 C	Torn Lettuce
½	Cucumber, Chopped
3	Ripe Tomatoes, Sliced
¼ C	Fat-Free Vinaigrette
4 T	(1 oz) Crumbled Feta Cheese
	Freshly Ground Pepper

DIRECTIONS

1. Combine lettuce, cucumber, tomato, and vinaigrette; toss.
2. Sprinkle each serving with 1 tablespoon feta cheese; sprinkle with freshly ground pepper, if desired.

Yield: *4 (1¼ Cup) Servings*
Per Serving: *Calories 68; Fat 4.8 g; Carbs 5.3 g*

Chicken Pasta Salad

INGREDIENTS

8 oz	Spiral Pasta
2 C	Cubed Cooked Chicken Breasts
1 can	(8 oz) Sliced Water Chestnuts, Drained
1 box	(10 oz) Frozen Drained Snow Peas, Thawed
⅓ C	Thinly Sliced Green Onions
½ C	Chopped Celery
	Salt and Pepper to Taste

DIRECTIONS

1. Cook pasta according to directions on package omitting oil; drain.
2. Combine pasta with remaining ingredients and toss with Dressing (see recipe below).
3. Refrigerate before serving.

DRESSING

¼ C	Non Fat Plain Yogurt
3 T	Lite Soy Sauce
1 T	Sherry

Mix all ingredients together.

Yield: *6 Servings*
Per Serving: *Calories 269; Fat 3.7 g*

Carrot Raisin Chicken Salad

INGREDIENTS

2 C	Shredded, Peeled Carrots
½ C	Thin Slices Green Bell Pepper (App. 4)
¼ C	Light Mayonnaise
½ C	Golden Raisins
2 T	Lemon Juice
1 T	Water
1 T	Sugar
¼ tsp	Dried Ginger
	Lettuce
2 C	Cubed Cooked Chicken Breasts

DIRECTIONS

1. Place carrots, raisins, water, and ginger in a 1½ quart casserole. Cover with lid. Microwave on high four minutes or until carrots are crisp tender.
2. Add chicken and green pepper.
3. Blend mayonnaise, lemon juice, and sugar together in a small bowl. Pour over carrot mixture; toss to coat ingredients. Refrigerate for two hours.
4. Arrange lettuce leaves on serving platter and mound chicken mixture in center.

Yield: *4 Servings*
Per Serving: *Calories 250; Fat 7.2 g*

Turkey and Broccoli Pasta Salad

INGREDIENTS

12 oz	Tri-Colored Pasta
3 C	Cubed Cooked Turkey Breast
2 T	Olive Oil
1	Yellow Bell Pepper, Seeded and Chopped
1 bag	(10 oz) Fresh Spinach
1 bunch	Green Onions, Chopped
1 bunch	Broccoli
2	Tomatoes, Peeled, Seeded, Chopped
	Salt and Pepper to Taste

DIRECTIONS

1. Cook pasta according to directions on package omitting oil; drain. Toss pasta with olive oil and chill.
2. Wash, stem, dry, and tear spinach into pieces.
3. Cook broccoli in microwave, covered, in a small amount of water for 4 minutes. Drain and cut into small pieces.
4. Assemble salad in large shallow dish. Using half of each ingredient, alternate layers with salt and pepper to taste in the following order: spinach, pasta, turkey, broccoli, green onions, yellow

pepper, and tomatoes. Repeat with remaining half of ingredients and top with Dressing (see below). Refrigerate.

DRESSING

2 C	Non-Fat Plain Yogurt
1½ tsp	Minced Garlic
⅔ C	Part Skim Ricotta Cheese
1½ tsp	Dried Basil
3 T	Tarragon Vinegar
1 tsp	Sugar
	Salt and Pepper to Taste

Mix all ingredients together.

Yield: *8-10 Servings*
Per Serving: *Calories 298; Fat 7.4 g*

INGREDIENTS

3 cans	(11 oz) White Corn (Shoe Peg)
1 jar	(2 oz) Diced Pimientos
1	Tomato, Chopped
1	Cucumber, Peeled and Chopped
1	Green Bell Pepper, Chopped
1	Bunch Green Onions, Chopped

DIRECTIONS

1. Combine all ingredients in bowl and toss with Dressing (see recipe below). Refrigerate and serve.

DRESSING

⅓ C	Non Fat Plain Yogurt
1 T	Vinegar
2 T	Fat Free Mayonnaise
½ tsp	Dry Mustard

Combine all ingredients, mixing well. Pour over corn mixture.

Yield: 10-12 Servings
Per Serving: Calories 63; Fat 0.5 g

INGREDIENTS

1 pkg	(16 oz) Broccoli Slaw
¼ C	Apple Juice
1	Red Delicious Apple, Chopped
⅓ C	Sugar
1	Green Onion, Chopped
¼ tsp	Salt
½ C	Cider Vinegar
¼ tsp	Pepper

DIRECTIONS

1. Combine broccoli slaw, apple, and green onion in a large bowl.
2. Combine vinegar, apple juice, sugar, salt, and pepper, stirring well.
3. Pour vinegar mixture over slaw mixture, and toss. Serve immediately, or cover and chill.

Yield: *9 (1 Cup) Servings*
Per Serving: *Calories 60; Fat 0.1g; Carbs 14.7 g*

Simple Coleslaw

INGREDIENTS

4 C	Packaged Coleslaw
⅓ C	Fat-Free Vinaigrette

DIRECTIONS

Combine coleslaw and vinaigrette.

Yield: 4 (1 Cup) Servings
Per Serving: Calories 27; Fat 0.1 g; Carbs 6.1 g

INGREDIENTS

1 T	Orange Juice
⅛ tsp	Salt
1 tsp	Vegetable Oil
2½ C	Chopped Broccoli Florets
1 tsp	Prepared Horseradish
1 tsp	Honey
¼ C	Finely Chopped Red Onion
2	Oranges, Sectioned

DIRECTIONS

1. Combine orange juice, vegetable oil, horseradish, honey and salt.

2. Place broccoli in a microwave-safe dish; cover and microwave at HIGH 2 to 3 minutes or until crisp-tender. Rinse with cold water, and drain.

3. Add broccoli, onion, and orange sections to orange juice mixture; toss well.

Yield: 2 (1 Cup) Servings
Per Serving: Calories 129; Fat 2.8 g; Carbs 25.9 g

Beans and Greens

INGREDIENTS

1 pkg	(10 oz) Mixed Salad Greens
1 can	(16 oz) No-Salt-Added Kidney Beans, Rinsed and Drained
1 can	(15 oz) Cannelloni Beans, Rinsed, Drained
1	Red Onion, Thinly Sliced
½ C	Reduced-Fat Olive Oil Vinaigrette

DIRECTIONS

Combine all ingredients; toss gently. Cover and chill, if desired.

Yield: *7 (1 Cup) Servings*
Per Serving: *Calories 143; Fat 3.1 g, Carbs 22.2 g*

INGREDIENTS

1 can	(15 oz) No-Salt-Added Black Beans, Rinsed and Drained
¼ C	Chopped Green Onions
¼ C	Frozen Whole-Kernel Corn, Thawed
½ C	Salsa
8 C	Shredded Romaine Lettuce

DIRECTIONS

1. Combine beans, green onions, corn, and salsa.
2. Spoon bean mixture over 2 cups shredded romaine lettuce.

Yield: *4 Servings*
Per Serving: *Calories 111; Fat 0.6 g; Carbs 21.3 g*

Desserts

Delicious Brownie Cakes

INGREDIENTS

1⅓ C	Vanilla Fat-Free No-Sugar-Added Ice Cream
1	Large Banana, Peeled and Sliced
4	(2" Square) Low-Fat Brownies (Such as Betty Crocker Sweet Rewards)
¼ C	Fat-Free Chocolate Syrup

DIRECTIONS

1. Scoop ⅓ cup ice cream into each of 4 dessert dishes; top evenly with banana.
2. Microwave brownies at HIGH 20 seconds or until warm.
3. Crumble brownies evenly over banana.
4. Top each serving with 1 tablespoon chocolate syrup.

Yield: *4 Servings*
Per Serving: *Calories 267; Fat 2.9 g; Carbs 58.6 g*

INGREDIENTS

4	(2″ Square) Low-Fat Brownies (Such as Betty Crocker Sweet Rewards)
8 tsp	Raspberry Fruit Spread
⅓ C	Chocolate Fudge Reduced-Fat Frosting

DIRECTIONS

1. Cut each brownie in half lengthwise. Spread 2 teaspoons fruit spread on bottom half of each brownie, and top each with remaining brownie half.

2. Melt frosting in microwave at HIGH 45 seconds or until thin and smooth. Pour frosting evenly over brownies, spreading on tops and sides of brownies.

Yield   *4 Servings*
Per Serving: *Calories 238; Fat 4.5 g; Carbs 48.6 g*

Strawberry Whip Parfaits

INGREDIENTS

2 C	Sliced Strawberries
2 C	Fat-Free Frozen Whipped Topping, Thawed
4	(1 oz) Slices Angel Food Cake

DIRECTIONS

1. Place strawberries in blender; process until smooth, stopping once to scrape down sides.
2. Fold strawberry puree into whipped topping. Tear angel food cake into pieces, and fold into strawberry mixture.
3. Spoon evenly into 4 parfait glasses; cover and chill 30 minutes.

Yield: *4 Servings*
Per Serving: *Calories 155; Fat 0.4 g; Carbs 33.9 g*

INGREDIENTS

1¼ C	Chocolate or Vanilla Fat-Free Ice Cream, Softened
16	Chocolate Wafer Cookies

DIRECTIONS

1. Spread 3 tablespoons ice cream onto flat side of 1 wafer cookie, and top with 1 wafer cookie.
2. Wrap each sandwich in heavy-duty plastic wrap, and store in freezer.

Yield: *8 (1 Sandwich) Servings*
Per Serving: *Calories 94; Fat 1.6 g; Carbs 18.2 g*

Chocolate Chip Frozen Yogurt

INGREDIENTS

½ C	Chocolate Chips
2 C	Vanilla Low-Fat Frozen Yogurt, Softened

DIRECTIONS

1. Stir chocolate chips into frozen yogurt.
2. Spoon into 4 dessert dishes.

Yield: *4 (½ Cup) Servings*
Per Serving: *Calories 196; Fat 4.0 g; Carbs 36.7 g*

INGREDIENTS

4 C	Sliced Strawberries
2 tsp	Sugar
1½ C	Frozen Reduced-Calorie Whipped Topping, Thawed
½ tsp	Almond Extract

DIRECTIONS

1. Sprinkle sugar over strawberries.
2. Combine whipped topping and almond extract.
3. Spoon strawberries evenly into 6 dessert dishes. Top evenly with whipped topping.

Yield: *6 Servings*
Per Serving: *Calories 72; Fat 2.5 g; Carbs 12.2 g*

Sugar Free Chocolate Pecan Brownies

INGREDIENTS

2 T	Cocoa Plus 1 Tablespoon Oil
⅔ C	Pecans
⅓ C	Margarine, Melted
½ C	Eggbeaters
2 T	Liquid Sweetener
1 C	Cake Flour
2 tsp	Vanilla
½ tsp	Salt
½ tsp	Baking Powder

DIRECTIONS

1. Preheat oven to 325 degrees.
2. Mix cocoa and oil.
3. Add melted margarine, sweetener, eggbeaters, vanilla, and pecans.
4. Blend all dry ingredients. Stir in liquid mixture.
5. Pour into an 8 x 8-inch square pan. Smooth batter.
6. Bake 20-25 minutes. Cut into 16 2-inch squares.

Yield: *16 Piece Servings*
Per Serving: *Calories 95; Fat 7 g; Carbs 6 g*

INGREDIENTS

1 C	Unsweetened Applesauce
½ tsp	Salt
2	Eggs
2 C	All-Purpose Flour
1 pkg	Sweet & Low (3⅓ Teaspoons)
1 tsp	Cinnamon
¼ C	Vegetable Oil
1 tsp	Baking Soda
½ C	Chopped Nuts (Optional)

DIRECTIONS

1. Preheat oven to 350 degrees
2. Cook 2 cups raisins in 2 cups water until almost dry.
3. ADD:
4. Mix all ingredients and bake in a 9 x 13-inch pan, greased and floured, at 350 degrees for 45 minutes.

Yield: 76 Cookies
Per Serving (2 Cookies): Calories 83; Fat 4 g; Carbs 10 g

Strawberry Cheesecake

INGREDIENTS

⅔ C	Graham Cracker Crumbs
3 T	Diet Margarine
1 pkg	Lemon Sugar Free Jello
1 C	Low-Fat Cottage Cheese
1 pkg	Dream Whip (Prepared as Directed)
5-6 pkg	Equal (or to Taste)

DIRECTIONS

1. Melt margarine in 8" X 8" dish.
2. Add crumbs. Mix and press. Bake at 350 degrees for 8 minutes. Cool.
3. Dissolve Jello with 1 cup hot water.
4. Add ¾ cup cold water and Equal. Refrigerate until slightly congealed.
5. Blend cottage cheese in blender until smooth. Add the thickened Jello and milk. Add this mixture to prepared Dream Whip. Mix well and pour over crumbs.

TOPPING

2 C	Fresh or Frozen Strawberries
2-3 tsp	Water
2 T	Low Calorie Strawberry Jelly
2 pkg	Equal

6. Mix water, Equal and topping.
7. Add sliced strawberries. Top each serving of
   cheesecake with topping.

Yield: 9 Servings
Per Serving: Calories 149; Fat 9 g; Carbs 12 g

Peanut Butter Balls

INGREDIENTS

¼ C	Peanut Butter
¼ C	Powdered Milk
¼ C	Raisins
4	Graham Crackers (2x2 Square), Broken in Pieces
1 tsp	Vanilla
Dash	Cinnamon

DIRECTIONS

1. Cream peanut butter with 2 tablespoons milk until well blended. Add remaining ingredients. Mix well.
2. Drop on aluminum foil or wax paper in balls about 1 inch in diameter. Place in freezer until ready to serve.

Yield: *16 Balls (2 Per Serving)*
Per Serving: *Calories 68; Fat 2 g; Carbs 3 g*

Brownies

INGREDIENTS

6 T	Light Margarine
1 C	Flour
4 T	Cocoa
4	Egg Whites
½ C	Sugar
1 tsp	Vanilla
1 C	Light Brown Sugar

DIRECTIONS

1. In cup, melt margarine and cocoa together in microwave. Combine with remaining ingredients, stirring until well mixed.

2. Pour batter into a 9x9x2-inch baking pan coated with no stick cooking spray and dusted with flour. Bake at 350 degrees for approximately 30 minutes.

Yield: *25 Squares*
Per Serving: *Calories 85; Fat 1.5 g*

Oatmeal Cookies

INGREDIENTS

1½ C	Flour
¼ C	Skim Milk
¼ C	Light Brown Sugar
2	Egg Whites
½ C	Sugar
1 tsp	Vanilla
1 tsp	Cinnamon
1½ C	Old-Fashioned Oatmeal
¼ tsp	Baking Soda
½ tsp	Baking Powder
½ C	Raisins
½ C	Chopped Pecans
½ C	Canola Oil

DIRECTIONS

1. In large bowl, combine flour, brown sugar, sugar, cinnamon, baking powder, and baking soda; set aside.

2. In another bowl, combine oil, milk, egg whites, and vanilla. Stir into dry ingredients, mixing well. Stir in oatmeal, raisins, and pecans.

3. Drop by rounded spoonfuls 1-inch apart on baking sheet coated with no stick cooking spray. Bake at 400 degrees for 10 to 12 minutes. Remove cookies to waxed paper to cool.

Yield: 4 Dozen Cookies
Per Serving (1 Cookie): Calories 75; Fat 3.2 g

Praline Meringues

INGREDIENTS

½ C	Dark Brown Sugar
¼ tsp	Lemon Juice
¼ C	Sugar
½ tsp	Vanilla
3	Egg Whites
½ C	Finely Chopped Pecans
½ tsp	Cream of Tartar

DIRECTIONS

1. Combine both sugars together.
2. In mixer, beat egg whites and cream of tartar until stiff
3. Beat in 1 tablespoon sugar mixture at a time, alternating with drops of lemon juice and vanilla. Beat until stiff and glossy. Fold in pecans.
4. On baking sheets lined with brown paper, drop by heaping teaspoons. Bake at 250 degrees for 45 minutes. (Meringue will spread during baking.)

Yield: 36 Meringues
Per Serving (1 Meringue): Calories 28; Fat 1 g

No Bake Cookies

INGREDIENTS

½ C	Graham Cracker Crumbs
2 T	Cocoa
2½ C	Old Fashioned Oatmeal
½ C	Skim Milk
1½ C	Sugar
½ C	Light Margarine
½ C	Peanut Butter
1 tsp	Vanilla

DIRECTIONS

1. In bowl, combine graham cracker crumbs and oatmeal. Set aside.
2. In saucepan, stir sugar, cocoa, milk, and margarine over medium heat until dissolved. . Bring mixture to boil and cook for 2 minutes. Remove from heat.
3. Stir in peanut butter and vanilla until well combined.
4. Quickly blend in cracker mixture. Beat by hand until thickens (few minutes).
5. Drop by teaspoon onto waxed paper. Refrigerate until firm and store in refrigerator.

Yield: 5 Dozen Cookies
Per Serving (1 Cookie): Calories 56; Fat 2.2 g

Extra Information

Herbs & Spices

Basil　　　　Compliments recipes with tomatoes or tomato sauce.

Bay Leaf　　　Adds nicely to soups, stews, and marinades.

Celery Seed　Adds flavor to soups and stock.

Chives　　　　Can be substituted for raw onion in any recipe.

Garlic　　　　Excellent in southern vegetables, soups, meats, and tomato based recipes.

Mustard (Dry)　Adds spice to sauces or over roast chicken.

Oregano　　　Good in tomato based dishes.

Paprika　　　Mild pepper, adds color to dishes.

Rosemary　　Excellent seasoning for poultry.

Tarragon　　　Goes well with poultry dishes.

Thyme　　　　Combines well with Bay leaves in soups.

Cinnamon　　Important in dessert preparation.

Cumin　　　　A staple spice in Mexican foods.

Chili Powder   Used for a highly spiced flavor
(Remember many commercial chili
powders are 40% salt and 20%
additives. Look for pure ground chili
powder.)

Peppercorns   Green, red, white, and black
peppercorns are available on the
market. Excellent added to almost
any dish.

Marjoram   Used in tomato dishes, eggplant,
zucchini, lima beans, and eggs.
Add to Meats for a flavor similar to
oregano.

Other Seasonings

Tomato Salsa Excellent for added zest to any dish.

Vinegars Balsamic, champagne, rice, malt, and red wine vinegar are just a few of the varieties available. Enhances salads, vegetables, and many cold meat dishes.

Liquid Smoke Excellent to add a hickory flavor to meats and vegetables.

Lemon Juice Fresh squeezed adds zest to salads and marinades.

Reduced Sodium Soy Sauce Reduces sodium. Good in stir fries and marinades.

Hot Sauces Adds a hot spiced flavor to soups, vegetables and marinades.

Butter Substitutes Enables one to enjoy a buttery flavor without the concentrated fat calories. Read labels to compare sodium content.

Lite Dressings (Italian & Catalina) Excellent marinade for meats, fish, and poultry.

Gumbo File* Good in soup and vegetable dishes as a thickening and spice.

Curry Powder	Use in sauces to baste fish and chicken, or in cheese dishes.
Fennel Seed	Sprinkle on top of breads before baking. Excellent to season broiled fish.
Sesame Seed	Sprinkle on breads before baking. Sprinkle on noodles, vegetables, and fish.
Parsley	Use as a garnish or add to rice, pastas, soups, stews, vegetables, fish, poultry, salads, and dressing.

Fresh spices have a more pungent flavor than dried. To enhance the flavor of dried spices, crush with spice mallet before using.

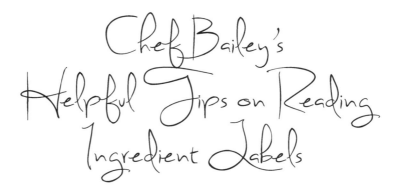

Chef Bailey's Helpful Tips on Reading Ingredient Labels

There is much confusing information concerning labels and how to read labels. We would like to help simplify the process to help you understand label reading and be prepared to make good nutritional choices. Let's look at the calories on a food label.

EXAMPLE: FOOD LABEL

Beef & Sauce Ingredients:

Tomatoes, beef broth, mushrooms, tomato paste, onion, red wine, starch, parmesan cheese, sugar, natural and artificial flavorings, chicken fat, hydrolyzed plant protein, salt, spices, vegetable, oil, citric acid & garlic.

Spaghetti Ingredients:

Cooked spaghetti and vegetable oil.

Nutritional Data:

Serving Size	9.0 oz
Servings Per Container	1
Calories	210
Protein	13 gm
Carbs	26 gm
Fat	4 gm
Sodium	770 mg
Potassium	550 mg

Percentages of US Daily Allowances (US RDA)

Protein	20
Riboflavin	10
Vitamin A	25
Niacin	10
Vitamin C	20
Calcium	8
Thiamine	10
Iron	*

* Contains less than 2% of the U.S. RDA of this nutrient.

Calories are listed Per Serving. Be sure to determine the number of servings provided per container, Many canned and frozen foods have two (2) or more servings per container. Not only must we look at more than just calories, but where they come from.

Food labels do not tell you how many calories come from fat. To find out, you must first look at the number of grams of fat on the label.

EXAMPLE:

4 gms fat x 9 calories per gm - 36 gms

210 calories   210 calories = 17% fat

The product should not exceed more than 30% of its calories from fat. Also note the source of fat. In this case, chicken fat is a source of fat and considered a saturated fat, increasing cholesterol. Cutting back on fat can help you control your weight and lipid levels.

Depending on your caloric requirements, your fat allowance will vary. You must first determine the amount of calories to maintain ideal weight. No more than 30% of your calories should come from fat.

EXAMPLE:

Total Calories	Calories From Fat Per Day	Max Grams Fat Per Day
1500	450	
50 gins		
(1500x30%)		
(450/9)		

CHOLESTEROL is not always listed on the label. When listed, it is in milligrams Per Serving or milligrams per 100 grams. Remember, your intake of cholesterol should not exceed 300 mg per day.

SODIUM is listed in milligrams. A safe and adequate intake is 3000-4000 milligrams per day (3-4 gms).

RDA'S are standards used in food labeling recommending proper amounts of vitamins and minerals to maintain health. For further analysis of your nutritional health, check with a registered licensed dietitian.

INGREDIENT LIST

Ingredients are listed in order of quantity. Beware of products which list fat or sugar as one of the first ingredients. Remember, fat can be listed in many ways: lard, butter, chicken fat, margarine, oil, or shortening.

DIETETIC FOODS

May not be low in calories. Many times sugar is removed from a product and extra salt or fat may be added. "Sugar Free", "Part Skim", "Non-Dairy", "Low Butterfat" or "Lite" does not necessarily mean a food is low-calorie or low-fat.

The following is a list of definitions that will enable you to make better food choices:

Extra Lean: No more than 5% fat by weight not by calories.

Leaner: 25% or less fat by weight than the regular product.

Sugar Free: Contains no table sugar (sucrose); however, may have fructose, corn syrup, honey, sorbital, or other sweeteners. Not always low in calories.

Sodium Free: No more than 5 mg Per Serving.

Very low sodium: No more than 140 mg sodium Per Serving.

Reduced sodium: 25% less sodium than regular product.

No salt added/Salt free: No salt added in processing; however, could have natural sodium or sodium from other products added.

Low in calories: No more than 40 calories Per Serving.

SUPERMARKETING

Dairy Foods: Use low-fat yogurt instead of mayonnaise or sour cream in dishes.

Part skim mozzarella, string cheese, low-fat ricotta and the many "lite" reduced calorie cheeses help us.

Low-fat versions of milk, buttermilk, cottage cheese, and yogurts are good nutritional values.

Meats: Select lean cuts: round steak, flank steak, tenderloin, loin chops, ground round. Use the "select" or diet lean cuts.

Limit meats high in saturated fats such as liver, bacon, ribs, sausage and duck. Venison is considered a lean meat.

Fresh Fish and Poultry: Buy skinless chicken or remove skin before cooking. One-half of the calories in chicken are from the skin.

Fish from deep waters are excellent sources of the omega-three (3) fatty acids which aid in lowering cholesterol levels. Examples are: salmon, sable fish, sea trout, bluefish, and mackerel. Catfish is a southern favorite much lower in saturated fat than beef and pork, supplying smaller amounts of omega-3 fatty acids.

Most pre-breaded chicken and turkey are usually high in sodium and fat.

Lean fresh ground turkey or chicken is an excellent substitute for ground beef.

Produce: Fresh vegetables are always a good choice. Be careful of added sodium.

Remember, skins of fruits, vegetables, and seeds are god sources of fiber.

Fruits and vegetables are good sources of Vitamin A and C.

Breads/Cereals: Look for "whole wheat" or "whole grain" at the beginning of the label.

Choose cereals with at least 2 grams of fiber Per Serving. Select cereals with less than 2 grams of fat Per Serving.

Sugar in many cereals is extremely high. Do not exceed 8 grams Per Serving. Use enriched breads. The "lite" breads can help cut calories.

Fats: The softer the margarine the better. Use only margarine or oil with unsaturated fats. (Example: corn oil and cottonseed.) Light mayonnaise has about 1.2 the calories of regular.

Use diet dressings to cut fat calories. May be used as a marinade for meats and poultry. Reduced calorie margarines can save calories.

Frozen Foods: Purchase frozen poultry and fish without breading to lower fat and sodium. Do not use frozen vegetables in sauces. Plain frozen is a good choice.

Look for frozen dinners with less than 30% of the calories from fat and less than 800 mg of sodium.

Frozen fruit juices are often less expensive than the prepared juice.

Deli: Sliced lean turkey, roast beef, and ham are good choices.

Lean ham or Canadian bacon are good choices to season southern vegetables to lower fat versus using bacon drippings and ham hocks.

Turkey or chicken wieners are still high fat and high in sodium-limit their use.

Processed lunch meats should be 95% fat free.

Packaged Products: Read labels—palm, palm kernel, and coconut oil are high in saturated fats and should be avoided.

Graham crackers, animal crackers, and gingersnaps have less fat and sugar than most other cookies.

Microwave popcorn is usually high fat and/or high sodium.

Thick unsalted pretzels are a better snack than most chips.

Most prepackaged mixes are high in sodium.

MICROWAVE, COOKING, CHART FOR VEGETABLES

Cooking vegetables in the microwave is the best way to preserve nutrients and flavor, and often the quickest way to cook them. Cook all the vegetables at HIGH power in a baking dish covered with wax paper. If you use plastic wrap to cover the dish, be sure to turn back one corner to allow steam to escape.

Food	Microwave Cooking Time	Special Instructions
Asparagus, 1 Lb	6-7 min	Add ¼ C water
Beans, green, 1 Lb	14-15 min	Add ½ C water
Broccoli spears, 1 Lb	7-8 min	Arrange in a circle, spoke-fashion, with flowerets in center; add ½ C water
Carrot Slices, 1 Lb	9-10 min/stand 2 min	Add ¼ C water
Cauliflower Flowerets, 1 Lb	7-8 min/stand 2 min	Add ¼ C water
Corn on the Cob		Arrange end-to-end in a circle; add ¼ C water
2 large ears	5-9 min	
3 ears	7-12 min	
4 ears	8-15 min	
Onions, peeled and quartered, 1 Lb	6-8 min	Add 2 T water
Peas, green, shelled 1 pound (about 1½ C)	6-7 min	Add 2 T water
Potatoes, baking/sweet, medium		Pierce skins and arrange end-to-end in a circle; let stand 5 minutes after cooking
1 potato	4-6 min	
2 potatoes	7-8 min	
4 potatoes	12-14 min	

New potatoes	8-10 min	pierce if unpeeled; add ¼ C water
Spinach, 10-oz pack	2-3 min	Wash leaves before cooking
Squash, Yellow/Zucchini, 1 Lb, slices (4 medium)	7-8 min	Add ¼ C water
Squash Acorn, 2 Lb (2 medium)	9-10 min	Pierce skins
Turnips, 1¼ Lb, peeled and cubed (4 medium)	10-12 min	Add ¼ C water

EQUIVALENTS

3 tsp	1 T
4 tsp	¼ C
5⅓ T	⅓ C
8 T	½ C
10⅔ T	⅔ C
12 T	¾ C
16 T	1 C
2 C	1 Pt
4 C	1 Qt
4 Qt	1 G
16 oz	1 Lb
32 oz	1 Qt
8 fl oz	1 C
1 fl oz	2 T

METRIC EQUIVALENTS

The recipes that appear in this cookbook use the standard United States method for measuring liquid and dry or solid ingredients (teaspoons, tablespoons, and cups). The information in the following charts is provided to help cooks outside the U.S. successfully use these recipes. All equivalents are approximate.

Equivalents for Different Types of Ingredients

A standard cup measure of a dry or solid ingredient will vary in weight depending on the type of ingredient. A standard cup of liquid is the same volume for any type of liquid. Use the following chart when converting standard cup measures to grams (weight) or milliliters (volume).

Table Next Page...

Standard Cup	Fine Powder (ex. Flour)	Grain (ex. Rice)	Granular (ex. Sugar)	Liquid Solids (ex. Butter)	Liquid (ex Milk)
1	140g	150g	190g	200g	240 ml
¾	105g	113g	143g	150g	180 ml
⅔	93g	100g	125g	133g	160 ml
½	70g	75g	95g	100g	120 ml
⅓	47g	50g	63g	67g	80 ml
¼	35g	38g	48g	50g	60 ml
⅛	18g	19g	24g	25g	30 ml

Liquid Ingredients by Volume

¼ tsp	=						1 ml
½ tsp	=						2 ml
1 tsp	=						5 ml
3 tsp	=	1 T	=		½ fl oz	=	15 ml
		2 T	=	⅛ C	1 fl oz	=	30 ml
		4 T	=	¼ C	2 fl oz	=	60 ml
		5⅓ T =		⅓ C	3 fl oz	=	80 ml
		8 T	=	½ C	4 fl oz	=	120 ml
		10⅔ T	=	⅔ C	5 fl oz	=	160 ml
		12 T	=	¾ C	6 fl oz	=	180 ml
		16 T	=	1 C	8 fl oz	=	240 ml
		1 Pt	=	2 C	16 fl oz	=	480 ml
		1 Qt	=	4 C	32 fl oz	=	960 ml
					33 fl oz	=	1000 ml = 1 L

Dry Ingredients by Weight
(To convert ounces to grams, multiply the number of ounces by 30.)

1 oz	=	$^1/_{16}$ Lb	=	30g
4 oz	=	¼ Lb	=	120g
8 oz	=	½ Lb	=	240g
12 oz	=	¾ Lb	=	360g
16 oz	=	1 Lb	=	480 g

Length
(To convert inches to centimeters, multiply the number of inches by 2.5)

1"	=					2.5 cm
6"	=	½'	=			15 cm
12"	=	1'	=			30 cm
36"	=	3'	=	1 yd	=	90 cm
40"	=					100 cm = 1m

Cooking/Oven Temperatures

	°F	°C	Gas Mark
Freeze Water	32 F	0 C	
Room Temperature	68 F	20 C	
Boil Water	212 F	100 C	
Bake	325 F	160 C	3
	350 F	180 C	4
	375 F	190 C	5
	400 F	200 C	6
	425 F	220 C	7
	450 F	230 C	8

Chef Bailey's Cherished Recipes Made Healthier

HANDY SUBSTITUTIONS

Ingredient Needed	Substitute
BAKING PRODUCTS	
1-cup self-rising flour	1-cup all-purpose flour, 1-teaspoon baking powder, and ½ teaspoon salt
1-cup cake flour	1-cup minus 2-tablespoons all-purpose flour
1-cup all-purpose flour	1-cup plus 2-tablespoons cake flour
1-cup powdered sugar	1-cup sugar and 1-tablespoon cornstarch (processed in food processor)
1-cup honey	1¼ cup sugar and ¼-cup water
1-teaspoon baking powder	¼-teaspoon baking soda and ½-teaspoon cream of tartar
1-tablespoon cornstarch	2-tablespoons all-purpose flour
½-cup chopped pecans	½-cup regular oats, toasted (in baked products)
1-ounce (square) unsweetened chocolate	3-tablespoons cocoa and 1-tablespoon butter or margarine
EGGS AND DAIRY PRODUCTS	
2-large eggs	3-small eggs

1-cup fat-free milk	½-cup evaporated fat-free milk and ½-cup water
1-cup plain yogurt	1-cup buttermilk
1-cup fat-free sour cream (for cooking)	1-cup fat-free yogurt and 1-tablespoon corn starch

VEGETABLE PRODUCTS

1-pound fresh mushrooms, sliced	1 (8-ounce) can sliced mushrooms, drained or 3-ounces dried
1-medium onion, chopped	1-tablespoon instant minced onion or 1-tablespoon onion powder
3-tablespoons chopped shallots	2½-tablespoons chopped onion or 1-tablespoon chopped garlic

SEASONING PRODUCTS

1-tablespoon chopped herbs	1-teaspoon dried herbs or ¼-teaspoon powdered herbs
1-garlic clove	¼-teaspoon garlic powder or 1-teaspoon bottled minced garlic
1-tablespoon dried orange peel	1½-teaspoons orange extract
1-teaspoon ground allspice	½-teaspoon ground cinnamon and ½-teaspoon ground cloves

ALCOHOL

2-tablespoons amaretto	¼ to ½-teaspoon almond extract
2-tablespoons dry sherry or bourbon	1 to 2-teaspoons vanilla extract
¼-cup or more white wine	Equal measure of apple juice or chicken broth
¼-cup or more red wine	Equal measure of red grape juice or cranberry juice

26524354R00123

Made in the USA
Lexington, KY
06 October 2013